KNOW WHO YOU ARE

LIVE LIKE IT MATTERS

Books by Tim Tebow

Through My Eyes

Shaken

Shaken Bible Study

Shaken Bible Study DVD

TIM TEBOW

KNOW WHO YOU ARE

LIVE LIKE IT MATTERS

A HOMESCHOOLER'S INTERACTIVE GUIDE
TO DISCOVERING YOUR TRUE IDENTITY

WITH A. J. GREGORY

WATERBROOK

Know Who You Are. Live Like It Matters.

Details in some anecdotes and stories have been changed to protect the identities of the persons involved.

Trade Paperback ISBN 978-0-7352-8994-9
eBook ISBN 978-0-7352-8995-6

Cover design by Kristopher K. Orr; cover photography by Bryan Soderlind

Published in the United States by WaterBrook, an imprint of the Crown Publishing Group, a division of Penguin Random House LLC, New York.

Library of Congress Cataloging-in-Publication Data
Names: Tebow, Tim, 1987– author.
Title: Know who you are, live like it matters / Tim Tebow with A.J. Gregory.
Description: First Edition. | Colorado Springs, Colorado : WaterBrook, 2017.
Identifiers: LCCN 2016058025 (print) | LCCN 2017011091 (ebook) | ISBN 9780735289949 (pbk.) | ISBN 9780735289956 (electronic)
Subjects: LCSH: Success—Religious aspects—Christianity. | Identity (Psychology)—Religious aspects—Christianity. | Christian life.
Classification: LCC BV4598.3 .T43 2017 (print) | LCC BV4598.3 (ebook) | DDC 248.4—dc23
LC record available at https://lccn.loc.gov/2016058025

Printed in the United States of America
2017—First Edition

10 9 8 7 6 5 4 3 2 1

To the greatest teacher I ever had: Mom.

To the mom or dad who's reading this book with your child, always remember that one of the greatest investments you'll ever make is in your family.

Contents

A NOTE FROM TIM

You and I have something in common. We may share similar traits I don't know about, but here's what I do know: I was homeschooled, just like you! I can't tell you how much I appreciate my parents for making a personal investment in my education. One of the things I loved about being homeschooled was being able to focus on the things I was passionate about and how much time it left for things I loved, like sports and exercise.

Here's something you may not know: my mom and dad decided to homeschool my two brothers, my two sisters, and me before people even knew what homeschooling meant. At the time, some people thought they were nuts. Some wondered if homeschooling was even legal! But despite the challenges they faced, it was worth it. Mom and Dad's careful and thoughtful instruction helped educate my siblings and me. Each one of us was even blessed to receive a college scholarship!

I know being homeschooled may not be the easiest thing in the world, so I wanted to write a book just for you. I'd like to encourage you in your studies by offering some lessons I've learned in my personal journey, lessons I want you to be a part of. I want this book to be about you: digging deep to find out who you are and what that means in real life.

You may or may not know this already, but writing is powerful. In fact, an esteemed professor of psychology at the University of Texas at Austin studied the impact of journaling. Through a handful of studies, this expert found that expressive writing in a personal and meaningful way positively impacts health, well-being, and self-development. It can put us in a better mood. It can help us process tough situations. It can challenge us to make good changes. It can pave the way for a more impactful future.

Knowing how journaling can be a great tool for self-reflection, I decided to write *Know Who You Are. Live Like It Matters.* just for homeschool students. You may think you don't like writing or that it doesn't come easy for you. That's okay! As we travel together through the course of this book, writing will become easier. And you may even discover it's one of your passions!

Here's what you'll find in the following pages. Each week for the next thirty-six weeks, I offer a verse from the Bible and a lesson that helps illustrate that verse. Each teaching ends with a section titled "In Your Own Words." This is your opportunity to reflect on what you've learned. You can connect what I talk about with what's going on in your life. Use my questions as prompts to fuel your thoughts.

This Guide Is Set Up in Four Parts with Nine Lessons Each

Part 1: Who Are You? (You'll learn about the source of your identity, Jesus Christ.)

Part 2: Don't Sweat It; God's Got It (You'll uncover guidance when the going in life gets tough.)

Part 3: Others Matter (Relationships are important. You'll understand why.)

Part 4: Live Bigger (You'll learn why and how to live in a way that impacts eternity.)

Here Are Some Helpful Tips to Know as You Get Started

- Don't think too hard before you write. Just start writing and see what comes.
- This journal will not be subject to grading. There are no wrong or right answers.
- Be sure to record your thoughts in complete sentences.
- Write from the heart. I recommend you take a minute to pray before you begin writing.
- Make it a goal to write in all or at least most of the space available. If you need more room, awesome! Ask your parents for a notebook or journal to record additional thoughts you may have.

Just for Parents

I am so grateful you have decided to use this guide as part of your children's lesson plans. As a homeschooled student, I know the effort, time, and work involved in choosing to educate your family. My parents were true pioneers in the homeschool movement. They took responsibility for educating their children before the general public even knew it was an option. I'm so grateful they were willing and committed to answering the call. And from the bottom of my heart, thank you for doing the same for your children!

The primary purpose of this book is to encourage students to reflect and put in writing thoughts, feelings, ideas, opinions, and experiences. While you may consider making some cursory adjustments to their entries (that is, if they make consistent spelling/grammar errors) or encouraging them to write more (if they need a push to hammer out more than one or two sentences), don't judge their ideas or their writing.

Finally, journal entries should be completed within thirty minutes. And it's best to set aside a specific day and time of the week for each lesson. Consistency is key!

I pray for God to honor your efforts, to give you strength when you're tired, grace when you need it, and wisdom throughout the process. I pray this journal inspires your children to dig deep with God and helps them find their purpose.

Part 1

Who Are You?

The world does not define you: Not the clothes you wear. Not the kind of music you listen to. Not the mistakes you've made. Not the trophies you've won. You are not defined by what others think of you, good or bad, or how many people follow or like you on Instagram or Snapchat or Facebook.

You are not defined by the talents you have or don't have.

There is only one thing, *one person,* who defines your identity. His name is Jesus Christ.

When you stop trying to follow the crowd, look a certain way, or do things just like everyone else, you can finally live in the unique design with which you were created. Because you are unique. You have value. And you matter!

When you let God rule your heart and your life, you can begin to live at your best. Isn't that what we all want? To be what God created us to be? To live out the dreams He planted in our hearts even before we were born?

The only way you can begin to do this is to know *whose* you are.

When you are secure in your identity, it will change you. It will give you purpose. It will help you handle tough times. It helps shape your future. It helps you see that you are not here by chance. And nothing can take that away!

Week 1

WHO ARE YOU?

KEY VERSE

For God so loved the world, that He gave His only begotten Son, that whoever believes in Him shall not perish, but have eternal life.

John 3:16

A few weeks before I started working on this book, I celebrated my spiritual birthday. Actually, I had so many things going on that I forgot. My mom reminded me. She even made me a cake! It's fun to celebrate birthdays with parties and presents, but you know what's even more important? Celebrating the day you were born into God's family. The day you asked Jesus into your heart.

Church was a huge part of my life growing up. At home, my parents taught me the importance of faith in Jesus and studied Scripture with me. In fact, one of the first Bible verses I memorized was John 3:16: "For God so loved the world, that He gave His only begotten Son, that whoever believes in Him shall not perish, but have eternal life."

This verse is the foundation of what it means to be a Christian. Maybe you've heard or read this verse hundreds of times. Maybe, like me, it's one of the first verses you memorized. Before you understand who you are, you have to know whose you are.

Let me break down this verse for you:

For God so loved the world. The world is not just every single one of the billions of people on this planet, but you! God so loved ______________________________ (write in your name here).

That He gave His only begotten Son. God loves you so much that He was willing to give up His own child for you.

That whoever believes in Him shall not perish, but have eternal life. You can live with God forever. All you have to do to be saved is to believe in Jesus (see Romans 10:9). This is what He wants for you. He loves you so much that He wants you to be a part of eternal life with Him!

I love these words because they're simple, clear, and packed with meaning.

I remember waking up one morning when I was six years old. Living on a forty-four-acre farm, my two brothers, two sisters, and I had a long chore list. There was always something to do. Mow lawns. Chase cows into the field. Lift hay bales. Chop wood. Weed the garden. That morning, before I set out to do my chores and while Dad was running the tractor, I told my mom I wanted to ask Jesus into my heart. It was the most important day of my life. In fact, my parents were so thrilled, we celebrated by eating dinner that night at one of the largest McDonald's in the world. (Though even at six, I should have known better than to chow down a Big Mac.) The next day, the festivities continued at Epcot.

So who are you? The dictionary defines *identity* as "who someone is, the name of a person, the qualities, beliefs, etc., that make a particular person or group different from others." I like to say that identity comes not necessarily from who we are but from *whose* we are.

If you believe in Jesus, you are a son or daughter of God. You are the object of His love. He has a plan and a purpose for your life (see Jeremiah 29:11). And He will never, ever leave or forsake you (see Hebrews 13:5).

IN YOUR OWN WORDS

1. Finish this thought: I am . . . (a child of God, loved, made with a purpose, and so on).

2. Describe your spiritual birthday. Where were you when you asked Jesus into your heart? Who was with you?

3. If you have never asked Jesus into your heart, I want to encourage you to do it right now with your mom or your dad. You can use your own words or read mine below:

   Dear Jesus, I know I am a sinner and need a Savior. Thank You that You died for me and rose again. I open the door of my heart and ask You to come in. Thank You for coming into my heart and forgiving my sins. Thank You that God is my Father and I am His child. Thank You that I have a home in heaven and that I will come and live with You someday. In Your name, amen.

SOMETHING TO THINK ABOUT

Jesus didn't save you because you're awesome: He saved you because He's awesome.

A LOVE WORTH KNOWING

KEY VERSE

But you, Lord, are a compassionate and
gracious God,
slow to anger, abounding in love and
faithfulness.

Psalm 86:15, NIV

I can remember a certain night like it was yesterday, being nine or ten years old and getting ready for bed.

- Hands washed? Check.
- Teeth brushed? Check.
- Room straightened up? Check.
- Pajamas on? Check.

As I waited for Mom or Dad to pray with me, I noticed them walking around the house, looking distracted. They talked to each other in hushed tones, serious expressions on their faces. I couldn't figure out what they were saying to each other, but I knew it was important. Then the phone rang. I knew I would get in trouble for eavesdropping if I was caught, but I did it anyway. I snuck as close as I could to where the phone was, hiding behind a wall on the other side of the room.

"No," I heard my parents say to the person on the line. "Your curfew is 9:00 p.m. sharp."

One of my older brothers had called, trying to weasel his way out of being home when he was supposed to be.

"I'm sorry, but the rules are the rules. You need to come home now." My parents were firm. And as the conversation went on, I could tell whoever was on the other end was doing their best to convince Mom or Dad to let them come home later.

My brother probably thought Mom and Dad were being mean, unreasonable, and way too strict. I know, because growing up I would get annoyed at certain rules they made and that when I didn't follow them, I had to endure the consequences.

That night, though, I saw a vivid picture of a parent's love for their child. I watched Mom and Dad, tears in their eyes, praying and hoping their son would come home soon. I watched how grieved they were, and how only when my brother walked through the door, safe and sound, did they experience relief. I knew in that moment that Mom and Dad weren't being mean; they were being loving parents. It's not that they wanted to keep their kids from doing something they wanted to do; they wanted to protect them, knowing what could happen.

A parent's love for a child can be pretty intense. Can you imagine how much more God loves us? He loves us so much He sent His Son to die for us. Think about this: God knows everything about you. He knows what you had for breakfast. He knows what you looked at on the computer the other day. He knows how many hairs are on your head. He knows your every thought. And guess what? His love for you never changes. Like the book of Psalms tells us, His love and faithfulness abound, always available. God will always love you, no matter what.

Knowing God loves us and wants the best for our lives helps us to stay grounded in our identity. If we feel unloved or unlovable, we can remind ourselves that we are children of God and that He loves us. Knowing this truth helps us to live at our best.

IN YOUR OWN WORDS

1. Who has taught you the most about love? How did this person show God's love through actions or words?

2. Do you feel worthy of God's love? Why or why not?

SOMETHING TO THINK ABOUT

God's love is pure. It never fails. It is unconditional. It is eternal. It is not motivated by personal gain. He just loves because He is Love.

Week 3

GOD'S GOT A PLAN

KEY VERSE

"For I know the plans I have for you," says the LORD. "They are plans for good and not for disaster, to give you a future and a hope."

Jeremiah 29:11, NLT

Since I was six years old, one of my dreams was to play in the NFL as a quarterback. I remember watching my two favorite teams back then, the Florida Gators and the Dallas Cowboys. *One day, I'll be running down the field, leading these teams in game-winning drives. Super Bowl, here I come!* But I did more than dream. I worked hard. I practiced. I trained.

I was proud to play college ball for the Gators. It was a dream come true. When we won a national championship, I was blown away hearing the tens of thousands of screaming fans who filled every inch of the stadium for that game. They stood on their feet, jumping up and down in a sea of orange and blue, celebrating our triumph over Ohio State. Confetti rained down. The band blasted a victory march. Cheerleaders did backflips. My teammates and I ran all over the field. It was madness! We won another national championship two years later and had another incredible time of celebration. During my college years, I won a number of awards, including the Heisman Trophy, an honor handed out each year to the most outstanding college football player in the country.

When I graduated, I was chosen to play quarterback for the Denver Broncos. Another dream come true! I was blessed to have some success on that team too, helping win a number of games in the fourth quarter, when things looked bleak. For a time, it seemed I was pretty popular. I got invited to a ton of famous parties and even the White House. My life wasn't perfect, but I truly believed I was smack in the middle of God's plans.

It wasn't that long after being celebrated by the world that everything changed. The plan I thought was solid started crumbling. After my season with the Broncos, I was traded to another team. They cut me a year later. After that, I was cut from two more teams before the season even started. Nobody in the NFL wanted me to play as a quarterback. Many told me I wasn't good enough. My dream seemed to die.

Battling disappointment, I struggled with God's plan for my life. Did He really have something good in mind? Did He know what He was doing?

You know what I've learned? We all go through highs and lows. And when we are grounded in whose we are, we have to trust that

God still has a plan, even when life isn't going that great. Even when something we hoped would happen doesn't. Even though our prayers don't get answered in the way we want.

God never promised us a perfect life; He promises us His presence. In Hebrews 13:5, He promises never to leave or forsake us. And He also promises that His plans for us are good and that somehow and in some way He will use them for a purpose greater than we can imagine (see Romans 8:28).

IN YOUR OWN WORDS

1. Are you struggling with something painful or disappointing? Write about the situation.

2. Now think about what you are going through in light of God's promise to give you a good future. How does that encourage you?

SOMETHING TO THINK ABOUT

Because our identity is secure in Jesus, we don't have to ride the roller coaster of life. We don't have to live up in the highs or down in the lows. No matter what happens we can live with confidence knowing we're on a solid foundation.

YOU MATTER

KEY VERSE

For we are His workmanship, created in Christ Jesus for good works, which God prepared beforehand so that we would walk in them.

Ephesians 2:10

"There's no way God could love me."

"I messed up too bad. God's given up on me."

"What's God going to do with me now?"

Since I was a freshman in college, I've visited about twelve American prisons, many of them multiple times, sharing with inmates the love and hope of Jesus. A few of those times I've had the opportunity to walk on death row, a space reserved for prisoners sentenced to die for committing horrific crimes. Some were sorry for what they'd done; others were hardened in their hearts. And almost all these prisoners I've met say something like the statements at the beginning of this lesson. Many of them think they just don't matter, especially because they've done bad things.

Thing is, they do matter to God.

God created all of us for a reason. He created us to be special. He created us for a purpose. Do you find this hard to believe? Many people do. Often we view ourselves based on how others see us, or the clothes we wear, or the car our parents drive, or where we live, or how many cool toys or electronic devices we have.

Some of us see ourselves in light of how we messed up. But if we think we matter based on those things, we're going to be in some pretty serious trouble. People who like you one day can change their minds the next. Styles fade. Gadgets break. Stuff doesn't last. And because we're sinners living in a fallen world, we're always going to make mistakes (that's why we need Jesus!). Here's a fact: you were created by Love, in love, and for love. This is not going to change.

Sometimes it's easy to think that we don't matter. *With billions of people on the planet, God must be too busy to be concerned with little ol' me.* But I have news for you, friend. You do matter! God does think about you! He does care about you!

A man named Paul, one of the earliest church missionaries, wrote our key verse: "For we are His workmanship, created in Christ Jesus for good works, which God prepared beforehand so that we would walk in them" (Ephesians 2:10). The Greek word for "workmanship" is *poiema,* from which we get the English word *poem.* It also can mean "masterpiece."

Think about this. Before you were even born, God wrote a beautiful poem about your life. He created you as a masterpiece, a breathtaking work of art. God's design for your life does not include meaningless or average things. You were created for more. You were created to make a difference. You were created with good things in mind. This means you are important. You are significant. You matter!

Remember last week when I talked about how no one wanted me as their quarterback? During those few years, I had to keep reminding myself over and over that God has a purpose. That He has a plan. Some days it was easy to believe; other days it was a struggle. And I learned that even though so-called experts or commentators told me in so many words that I didn't matter, God, through His Word, tells me I do. And that's what matters more!

IN YOUR OWN WORDS

Have you ever had a time when you were trying to be like someone else, only to discover that it wasn't working so well? Write about that experience and what you learned.

SOMETHING TO THINK ABOUT

You aren't an accident. . . . You weren't mass produced. You aren't an assembly-line product. You were deliberately planned, specifically gifted, and lovingly positioned on this earth by the Master Crafts-Man.

—Max Lucado, *God Thinks You're Wonderful*

Week 5

YOU + GOD = A WINNING TEAM

KEY VERSE For nothing will be impossible with God.

Luke 1:37

He is a teenager. The youngest of eight boys in his family. A red-haired runt who looks after his father's sheep, tending to them in green pastures. His older brothers are big shots. Strong and smart, they are soldiers in an army that defends their nation, Israel.

On the battlefield stands a contender who aims to destroy this army. His name is Goliath. This Special Forces soldier looms over thousands of his comrades who stand beside him. "Send someone to fight me," he roars. Silence rings out in the valley. No one wants to step forward.

Enter this teenage kid.

I'm sure you know the story of David and Goliath. It's a pretty famous one that's easy to take for granted because we've heard it so many times. You probably know that David volunteers to fight

Goliath. He presents himself before the king of Israel and says, "I'm up for the challenge. Send me." The king tries hard not to laugh. When other people hear about this boy's bold move, they think he's insane. No one believes in David. But he's persistent. He tells the king why he's the man for the job. "I've had to take care of my father's sheep. I've protected them against wild animals. I've killed lions and bears. I can do this." The king is not convinced.

But David knows something the king doesn't. This kid has faith. He has a personal relationship with God. A big God. A God with whom big things are possible. And David trusts that God has his back no matter what.

The king finally relents. While gracious about it, David refuses the king's offer of a suit of armor, a sword, and a shield to battle Goliath. This boy uses what's worked before. He faces a giant with a prayer and a sling.

Off David goes. Stopping at a stream before heading to the front line, the boy picks up five stones for his sling (see 1 Samuel 17:40). He puts them in his bag. Why five? Is David afraid that he wouldn't knock the giant down on the first, second, or even third try? No. David knows Goliath has four family members who are just as big, strong, and dominating. This boy has so much faith that God is on his side, that just in case these fellow bad boys happen to show up on the battlefield, he'd be ready to take them down too. Wow! I love this. What swag! What confidence in God!

We all know what happens next. Not caring that the army of Israel thinks he's a fool, not noticing some soldiers—maybe even a brother or two—are laughing at him, David draws back his sling and releases a stone like a missile. Goliath goes down. He is finished.

How does a shepherd believe he can crush a giant? Where does he get such confidence? Was it skill? A ton of practice? The power of positive thinking? Maybe all of those to an extent, but there's much more. David's deep faith in God is what gives him great courage. He knows God is more powerful than fear, doubt, and giants. He knows God will protect him. He knows God has been faithful and will be faithful again. And David knows that with God all things are possible.

IN YOUR OWN WORDS

Name a giant in your life. Write a story of how God can help you face that giant.

SOMETHING TO THINK ABOUT

With God, nothing is impossible. He has more ropes and ladders and tunnels out of pits than you can conceive. Wait. Pray without ceasing. Hope.

—John Piper, quoted in *The Christian Post*

Week 6

LOOK WHO'S WATCHING

KEY VERSE For the ways of a man are before the eyes
of the LORD,
and He watches all his paths.

Proverbs 5:21

"Hi, Mrs. Smith," I said to the woman hosting our family for lunch. "Thank you for having us over. You're such an amazing cook. I can't wait to see what you made us. Oh, and that's a real pretty dress you're wearing. You look beautiful!" At the end of this theatrical show of kindness, I flashed a wide grin, beaming from ear to ear. My game face was spot on.

"Why, Timmy, you are so, so sweet!" Mrs. Smith said, leaning down to pat me on the head. She turned to face my parents who were standing right beside me. "You two sure raised this boy right. You must be so proud of Timmy. What a fine young man!"

Cha-ching! Jackpot! Still smiling, I looked at Mom and Dad from the corner of my eye. I wanted to make sure they heard every word Mrs. Smith had said. A compliment from her meant another dollar to add to my growing collection of savings.

As I was growing up, my parents created for us five kids a rewards program called Daddy's Dollars. Every time someone outside our family said something nice about our character, Dad would give us a dollar. Sometimes he'd give us a real bill, other times a printed paper we could exchange for a prize in a chest of goodies or for privileges, like TV or computer time. We would also get dollars for doing extra chores.

My family is super competitive. It didn't matter if we were playing Monopoly or basketball; we each would do everything in our power to win. Even as the youngest of five, I was determined to get the most Daddy's Dollars. I tell you what, I worked really hard for compliments. I helped carry groceries. I always held the door open for someone. I was first to raise my hand to volunteer. And I did all these things in front of my parents.

And that was the problem.

When I was around nine or ten, I realized how empty it was to do nice things for a dollar, or a pat on the back, or any other material reward. I remembered one of the Bible verses I memorized growing up: "For the ways of a man are before the eyes of the Lord, and He watches all his paths." God is always watching us. He sees us doing the right thing. He sees us doing the wrong thing. He sees us doing nothing.

Who are you when no one is watching?

What do you do or don't do when your parents, your youth group leader, or an older sibling isn't around?

Do you do the right thing because it's simply the right thing to do?

Imagine your life is a movie. And God is sitting in heaven, watching on the edge of His seat as your story, every scene, every minute, unfolds. Are you the underdog? The hero? The villain? I want you to know God is with you, and He is always rooting for you to make the right choices.

When we start living and acting like God's eyes are always watching, I can guarantee we will start living a little differently. We realize we want to please Him more than anyone. And even if no one notices that we gave our allowance away to someone who doesn't have much, or picked up that piece of trash on the sidewalk, or said a kind word to someone who seemed to be hurting, it doesn't matter. It's more important to do things because God's watching. While it's nice to be rewarded with stuff, it's more fulfilling to please our heavenly Father.

IN YOUR OWN WORDS

1. How does it make you feel to know that God's eyes are always on you?

2. Write a prayer asking God for help to do the right thing even when it's hard.

SOMETHING TO THINK ABOUT

Integrity: when no one will ever know the good or right thing you do but you do it anyway.

Week 7

THE WHY BEHIND THE RIGHT THING

KEY VERSE

People with integrity walk safely,
but those who follow crooked paths will slip and fall.

Proverbs 10:9, NLT (2004)

Last week I talked about doing the right thing because God is watching. Now, thinking about the big picture, I wonder why you seek to do the right thing. What motivates you to tell the truth, or to obey your parents, or to treat others with respect? What inspires you to serve in your youth group, help your neighbor with her groceries, or check on that little kid who took a tumble on the playground?

I'll let you in on a little secret. If you do the right thing just to do the right thing, you're going to wear yourself out at some point. We should always do the right thing because we want to honor Jesus, because we want to be like Him in everything we think, say, and do. He is our motivation because He died for our sins. Jesus gave His life for us so we might live. One of my good friends who happens to be a pastor recently shared this story to help illustrate this principle.

Growing up, my friend and his brother received pretty awesome Christmas presents. One year their parents gave them each a beagle puppy. My friend's brother called his the Incredible Hulk. My friend named his little dog Daisy Duke. The puppies were bred to be hunting dogs, but they didn't do any hunting. These two brothers spoiled their dogs instead of training them.

One day, the two boys, their father, and their dogs went hunting. Daisy Duke took off near a river that looked frozen. Much to my friend's horror, the little dog stumbled upon a spot that wasn't frozen, and the little dog plunged into the icy waters, yapping for help before the current swept her downstream. My friend cried out from the shore, not sure what to do. Tears streaming down his face, he watched as Daisy Duke floated right by him, trapped under the ice. Crying uncontrollably, eyes fixed on his puppy imprisoned in the water, deprived of oxygen, minutes, even seconds away from death, he noticed his dad rushing out over the ice with his hunting gun. With all of his might, the man rammed the butt of his gun into the ice. Then in a split second he reached into the frigid waters and pulled Daisy Duke out by her neck. Just in the nick of time. The puppy was drenched, ice crystals forming on the edge of her fur. As she gasped for breath, my friend was beside himself. Tears of joy soaked his cheeks. Daisy

Duke survived, thanks to an incredible act of compassion and selflessness.

From that day forward, the little dog became a loyal companion to the boy's father, who until that moment never paid much attention to her. Wherever the man went, she followed. Whatever the man said, she did. Daisy Duke never, ever left his side.

Before inviting Jesus into our hearts, we are like Daisy Duke, trying to survive but trapped under ice, or in our case, sin. When we truly understand the sacrifice Jesus made on our behalf, we ought to become like that loyal dog: Following always after His footsteps. Being obedient to His Word. Honoring Him by loving, helping, and serving others.

This is why we seek to have integrity. This is why we build good character. This is why we do the right thing. Because Jesus did it first and our mission is to be like Him.

IN YOUR OWN WORDS

Write a letter to Jesus. Tell Him what it means that He died for your sins. Share how His sacrifice has changed or is changing the way you live and honor Him.

SOMETHING TO THINK ABOUT

There is always the danger that we may . . . just do the work for the sake of the work. It is a danger; if we forget to whom we are doing it. Our works are only an expression of our love for Christ.

—Mother Teresa, *Where There Is Love, There Is God*

YOUR WORD MATTERS

KEY VERSE

But let your "Yes" be "Yes," and your "No," "No."

Matthew 5:37, NKJV

When I was younger, I had a tight-knit group of guy friends at church. We did everything together. We hung out together. We played sports together. We went to youth group together. One day we came up with a unique saying, something shared in private among ourselves. Though I can't remember exactly what it was, I remember it was an acronym (a word or a name formed from the initial letters of the words in a phrase) of some sort. This word had a special meaning that only we knew. And we promised one another not to share it with anyone else.

The girls in our youth group quickly became curious. For a

while, they'd come up to us, one at a time, trying to sweet-talk their way into finding out what that word meant. They were pretty persistent. "Tell me," they each begged. "Please?" But we wouldn't. We would not go back on our promise to one another.

Well, I'll never forget the day one kid in our group blabbed our secret. I don't know why he did it. Probably because he had a crush on one of the girls and wanted to impress her. It's always tempting to do something dumb to show off for someone we really like. Looking back, it wasn't that big of a deal, and I definitely should have cut my friend some slack. But at the time I was so hurt that I didn't talk to him for a few days.

There's a reason the Bible tells us to let our yes be yes and our no be no. God keeps His word. And He expects us to. We've talked about this already, but one of the ways we live knowing our identity in Jesus is secure is to represent Him. And one way to do this is to only make promises we can keep.

If you say you're going to do something, do it. If you say you're going to commit to something, do it. I love what Ecclesiastes 5:2 tells us, "Don't talk before you think or make promises to God without thinking them through" (CEV). This verse reminds me how we are often quick to say something we don't mean. How many times have you said one or more of the following statements, whether to a person or to God, only to not follow through?

- "Of course I'll pray for you."
- "I'll call you later."

- "I promise, God, if You help me pass this test/answer my prayer exactly how I want/get me out of this mess, I'll be nicer to my little brother/go to church four times a week/ do every chore for a month without complaining."

There are many reasons we say things we don't mean or make promises we don't keep. We might be desperate. Or in a bind. Or want to get someone off our backs. We don't always have bad intentions in not following through on our word. Sometimes we just forget. Or we use a phrase we're so used to saying that we've forgotten what it really means.

Hey, I've been there. As a Christian I know how easy it is to tell someone, "Sure, I'll pray for you" and forget to do it. Years ago, the Holy Spirit convicted me for not praying for someone I'd promised to pray for. I didn't mean not to do it. It just slipped my mind. Keeping my word is important. And I strive to do this.

Today, if I meet someone who asks, "Timmy, would you please pray for my nephew who's really sick?" I either pray right on the spot or as I walk away after we have said good-bye.

If we live secure in our identity in Jesus, our words must matter. Let's mean what we say.

IN YOUR OWN WORDS

Complete the thoughts below.

1. By keeping my promises to my friends, I . . .

2. By keeping my promises to my parents, I . . .

3. By keeping my promises to God, I . . .

SOMETHING TO THINK ABOUT

Keep your word. Mean what you say. It matters to people, but more importantly, it matters to God.

Week 9

FAITH IS A MUSCLE—TRAIN IT!

KEY VERSE

Bind them [God's words] continually on
your heart;
tie them around your neck.
When you walk about, they will guide you;
when you sleep, they will watch over you;
and when you awake, they will talk to you.

Proverbs 6:21–22

As I was growing up and our family ate breakfast together each morning, we read verses from Psalms and Proverbs. Both of my parents required us to memorize a large number of Bible verses. To help us, Mom would put the verses to music in songs that she had made up. This was a pretty good strategy to "bind" God's words in my heart. It helped me remember Scripture for years to come. Even today, I catch myself humming a song Mom wrote from Psalms or Proverbs.

My parents didn't make us memorize Bible verses for the sake of simply loading our brains with more information. They were equipping us for our futures. Reading the Bible, meditating on it, and memorizing it fills our minds with what we need to grow as Christ followers. In 2 Timothy 3:16–17 we read, "Everything in the Scriptures is God's Word. All of it is useful for teaching and helping people and for correcting them and showing them how to live. The Scriptures train God's servants to do all kinds of good deeds" (CEV).

Even Jesus understood the power of God's Word. When He was tempted in the desert by Satan, He fought back by reciting Scripture (see Matthew 4; Luke 4).

What happens when we hide God's words in our hearts? We grow our faith. When we grow our faith, we root our identity deeper and deeper in whose we are. We become empowered with what we need so we can face the highs and lows of life.

Faith is like a muscle. The more you train it, the bigger it gets. As an athlete I know how important regular exercise is to the human body. To get stronger and faster, I have to work out. I have to condition my muscles. But training my faith is even more important. When we do this, we please God. In fact, the Bible says, "Without faith it is impossible to please Him" (Hebrews 11:6).

When you invest in your relationship with God—when you pray, when you study His Word, when you seek Him—your faith muscle grows. It gets bigger. The more you trust Him with the small things, the quicker you can trust Him with the big things.

Life is not always going to be easy. You might understand this already. There are always ups and downs. You can get psyched one day having made the soccer team and the next feel like a failure because you bombed a math test. When we exercise and grow our faith, we can deal with whatever comes.

So own your relationship with God. Remember, your faith is yours. It's not your parents'. It's not your friend's. It's not your coach's. It's not your pastor's. It's your own. Take it seriously. Take responsibility for it. And know that it's an ongoing journey.

As an athlete, I have to train all the time. I can't take a few weeks off just because I feel like it, because I'll get weak and slow. Similarly, we must invest in our faith every day. It's the only way we'll be able to tackle the mountains that may lie ahead.

IN YOUR OWN WORDS

Write down five goals that will draw you closer to God and deepen your faith. Include as part of your goals what it will take to achieve them. For example, your goal could be to spend fifteen minutes in quiet time in the morning before school. To do that, you might need to wake up twenty minutes earlier than you do now.

SOMETHING TO THINK ABOUT

The more you trust God for the little things, the more you can trust Him with the big things.

Part 2

Don't Sweat It; God's Got It

Not everything in life is easy. Tough times can throw us for a loop at any moment. This is why it's so important to stay rooted in whose we are. While we certainly need to believe in Jesus and live for Him during good times, we need to hold on to Him even more when we go through tough ones.

So when you're faced with doing something out of your comfort zone, when you feel unsure or not good enough, when you're struggling to do the right thing, when you feel like giving up because you've failed, *trust God.* He's always got a plan. And He will never give up on you. If you keep focused on whose you are, you will always have something unshakable to hold on to.

Week 10

WHEN WORDS HURT

KEY VERSE

For You formed my inward parts;
You wove me in my mother's womb.
I will give thanks to You, for I am fearfully
and wonderfully made;
wonderful are Your works,
and my soul knows it very well.

Psalm 139:13–14

The bleachers explode with cheering parents and students. It's loud, but I don't pay much attention. I'm focused.

I'm thirteen years old. I've just been invited to play spring ball for a varsity team.

This is my first live scrimmage. I don't care that the final score doesn't technically matter. To me, a game is a game. It always matters. And I'm determined to help my team score winning touchdowns. The guys have a few years on me, but I'm confident. I'm young but willing to prove my worth on the team. I feel good. Strong. Fast.

Let's do this.

I call the cadence. "Down. Set. Hut." The last word comes out of my mouth a little too high pitched for comfort. I ignore this and take the snap. One of the coaches, however, takes notice. He blares the whistle and storms toward me. I stop what I'm doing. Using coarse language I can't repeat, this coach uses some colorful words to tell me, "Stop acting like a little boy. Be a man." And after finishing his not-so-nice remarks with a "Bark it out next time!" he storms back off the field.

I didn't show it, but I was humiliated. This was my chance to man up. To prove to my teammates that I could play with the big boys. And in only a few seconds, my confidence fell straight to the ground like a bomb.

Words can hurt. Hurtful words are hard to hear coming from anyone, whether a sibling, friend, or bully, and even harder to hear from someone we look up to like a youth leader, coach, or teacher. You may have been on the receiving end of negative words. Maybe you were told you were good for nothing. Maybe someone made fun of your style. Maybe you're being picked on by someone who thinks you're too small, too big, too short, too tall, too this, or too that.

Hey, I've been blasted all over the Internet and face to face. People have told me that I was a terrible quarterback, that I couldn't play to save my life, and that I was a phony.

I'd like to think there's a way to keep you from being under the fire of hurtful words, but there isn't. So what can we do when someone speaks something cruel or negative to us? I've learned that regardless of what others say about us, it's more important to remember what God says about us. When we catch even a glimpse of how much God loves us, it changes how we think of ourselves. We can withstand hurtful words. We can be unmoved by mean-spirited or negative criticism.

Here are some key ideas from several Bible verses that have helped remind me of what God says about me. I pray they encourage you as well.

- I am fearfully and wonderfully made (see Psalm 139:14).
- I am a child of God (see Galatians 3:26).
- I am God's masterpiece (see Ephesians 2:10, NLT).
- God's hand is always upon me (see Psalm 139:5).
- As a child of God, I am a special treasure (see Exodus 19:5, NIV).
- God loves me with unfailing love (see Jeremiah 31:3, NLT).
- I am chosen by God (see 1 Thessalonians 1:4, NIV).

IN YOUR OWN WORDS

1. Describe a time someone said something that hurt your feelings. How did it make you see yourself?

2. Read and write down the scriptures I listed above. How can each one boost your self-worth based on what God says?

SOMETHING TO THINK ABOUT

What God knows about us is more important than what others think. When someone hurts you with words, remember whose you are. Remember that the God of the universe created you. Remember that you are His masterpiece. Remember that He has a purpose and a plan for your life. Remember that He loves you and always will, no matter what.

Week 11

FAILURE IS NOT FINAL

KEY VERSE

When you stumble and fall,
you get back up,
and if you take a wrong road,
you turn around and go back.

Jeremiah 8:4, CEV

No matter how smart, strong, fast, witty, knowledgeable, skilled, or talented we are, guess what? At some point in time, we are going to fail at something. I'm not trying to start this lesson with a downer. It happens to be true. In fact, some of the most successful people in this world have failed multiple times on their way to achieving remarkable things.

I'm guessing you probably know who Michael Jordan is. If you don't, he is the best basketball player of all time. I love what he said in one of his ads: "I've missed more than nine thousand shots in my career. I've lost almost three hundred games. Twenty-six times I've been trusted to take the game-winning shot and missed. I've failed over and over and over again in my life. And that is why I succeed." We're talking about a guy who helped his team win three consecutive NBA championships and then retired. Later Michael came out of retirement to win another three consecutive championships. Here's something else that's interesting. When he was a sophomore in high school, Jordan didn't even make the varsity basketball team.

Michael Jordan is not the only one who knows something about failure.

Henry Ford, founder of the successful Ford Motor Company, failed at five different business ideas before creating the Model T, a car that revolutionized the automobile industry.

Dr. Seuss, the author of one of my favorite books, *Green Eggs and Ham,* was rejected by twenty-seven different publishers while trying to publish his first book.

Abraham Lincoln didn't travel an easy path to get to the White House and serve as our sixteenth president. He lost eight elections, not to mention accumulating two business failures along the way. He said this: "My great concern is not whether you have failed, but if you are content with your failure."

Winston Churchill, prime minister of the United Kingdom during World War II, actually failed the sixth grade. He also failed the entrance exam to the military college Sandhurst three times. And before Churchill was appointed prime minster in 1940 when he was sixty-five years old, he "lost more elections than any other political figure in recent British history."*

And, of course, there's Thomas Edison. America's most well-known inventor was told as a boy that he was stupid. Before his death, he would hold 1,093 US patents and invent life-changing devices like the phonograph, incandescent light bulb, and movie camera. He invented the light bulb after reportedly ten thousand failed attempts and had this to say about it: "I have not failed 10,000 times. I have not failed once. I have succeeded in proving that those 10,000 ways will not work. When I have eliminated the ways that will not work, I will find the way that will work."†

There are many more men and women who have experienced failures yet changed the course of history.

Don't let failure stop you from being ambitious and trying new things. Every day is an opportunity to grow, to learn from your mistakes, to do something different. You might have failed yesterday. That's okay. It's more important to get back up. To try again. To keep at it.

Not making the team, not passing the test, or not scoring the goal isn't the worst thing that can happen. Not trying and not giving everything you have is.

---

* *Encyclopedia Britannica Online,* s.v. Winston Churchill, www.notablebiographies.com/Ch-Co/Churchill-Winston.html.

† Thomas Edison, quoted in Nathan Furr, "How Failure Taught Edison to Repeatedly Innovate," *Forbes,* June 9, 2011, www.forbes.com/sites/nathanfurr/2011/06/09/how-failure-taught-edison-to-repeatedly-innovate/#2e7d9ff138f5.

IN YOUR OWN WORDS

Write a story about someone who has experienced a number of failures. As he or she tried again and again, what happened?

SOMETHING TO THINK ABOUT

Failures, repeated failures, are finger posts on the road to achievement. One fails forward toward success.

—Charles F. Kettering, *The Reader's Digest*

Week 12

NOT GOOD ENOUGH

KEY VERSE

Before I formed you in the womb I knew you,
before you were born I set you apart.

Jeremiah 1:5, NIV

I remember it like it was yesterday. I'm twelve, maybe thirteen. I sit behind a desk with a handful of other students. The teacher holds in her hand a high stack of tests and starts passing them around the room, one by one. In a stern tone, she says, "Put all your personal belongings under your desk. Keep only your pencil out. You will have two hours to complete this test. Make sure to fill in your answers completely."

My stomach starts to churn. The teacher eyes the clock on the wall. It glares at me with a threatening look. "Okay. And your time starts now." The sound of papers rustling echoes throughout the room. I sweat nervously. There's no way around it. I do not like taking tests.

Even though we were homeschooled, Mom made us take standardized tests every year. She wanted an outside assessment of how we were doing. Also, hoping we would get scholarships to college, she and Dad wanted to make sure we were exposed to testing.

While sports came naturally to me, I struggled to read. When I was young, my parents determined I was dyslexic, which simply means I process things differently. I had a hard time reading books, writing essays, and taking timed tests. I would get frustrated easily. *Why can't I just pick up a book and read it like everyone else? Why does it have to take me hours and hours?* Going into high school, I wondered if I'd pass algebra or be able to take the SATs, let alone make it through college.

If you had told me when I was young that I'd not only graduate college but also maintain a 3.7 GPA, I'd have laughed in your face. I am so grateful for Susan Vanderlinde, my tutor growing up, whose knowledge and compassion made the learning process so much easier. She was a blessing!

Back to the testing day, I sat beside a kid from church. I'm going to tell you more about him in week 21, but for now know that he was picked on mercilessly for being short (by church kids no less!). As I leaned over the exam, slowly reading question after question, from the corner of my eye I noticed him zooming through each page. At the halfway mark, he put his pencil down. He was finished. Wow! People may have poked fun at this kid for his small stature, but he was a genius. Turns out, he received a nearly perfect score, while I had many wrong answers and barely finished in time.

Every one of us struggles with something. And that struggle can all too quickly influence us to think we're not good enough. I could have easily walked away from that classroom thinking, *I'll never be good enough at tests.* And that kid could have walked away from church many times thinking, *I'll never be good enough to fit in.*

If you struggle with not feeling good enough, know this: God knew about you even before you were born! When you came into existence, He gave you what it takes to fulfill a unique purpose. You may not be the quarterback of a team, a famous rock star, an award-winning actress, or an Olympic gymnast, but you have a special ability. And with God, that's always more than enough.

IN YOUR OWN WORDS

Sometimes when you feel down or struggle with feeling good enough, one of the best things to do is to encourage yourself. I bet it's easy for you to try to cheer up a friend or a sibling. But sometimes you're the one that needs the pick-me-up. Write a letter to yourself. Be positive and encouraging.

SOMETHING TO THINK ABOUT

If you are struggling with your self-worth, remember that the God of this universe created you and has a great plan for your life.

Week 13

FEAR, MEET LOVE

KEY VERSE

There is no fear in love; but perfect love casts out fear.

1 John 4:18

My dad, a missionary, is a man who has the most courage of anyone I've ever met. In 1985, he and my mom moved the family (nine-year-old Christy, seven-year-old Katie, four-year-old Robby, and one-year-old Peter) to the Philippines, a country on the western edge of the Pacific Ocean. Our family lived on the more remote southern island of Mindanao. Two years later they moved to Manila, where I was born.

The political landscape of the country was unstable. A lot of fights broke out between the Philippine government and the people. When I was only a week old, Dad watched, shocked, as armed rebel forces rolled down our streets in military tanks. Chaos broke out in the city streets. Gunfire rained down. People were running this way and that, scared out of their minds. Needless to say, Dad came back quickly to our house. We gathered some personal belongings and evacuated immediately, taking refuge in a hotel.

My mom recently told me that one time while Dad was preaching, someone holding a knife ran right behind where he was standing, holding his arm high in the air as if to attack Dad with the weapon. My father didn't even notice the guy. It took all of a few seconds before someone tackled the man holding the knife.

That's pretty scary stuff. My dad has countless stories of times he could have experienced fear. But he didn't. Why? Because he understood that God's perfect love for him is stronger than fear. Our key verse tells us that perfect love casts out fear. What does this mean?

God is perfect. His love is perfect. And God loves us perfectly. If we understand this truth, we realize that God is greater and more powerful than anything that might scare us.

Fear can be a powerful weapon. It can keep us from doing things that God wants us to do. We might not share Jesus with a kid in the neighborhood, because we're afraid she might think we're weird. We might not stand up for the kid who is being bullied, because we're afraid of what the bully might do to us. We might not try out for the church play or the local basketball team, because we're afraid we're not good enough.

Courage can help to overcome a fear, but love is what will conquer that fear. What fears overwhelm you? Are you afraid that others won't like you? Of looking silly? Of never fitting in? Of not passing the test? That you won't make friends at your new church or the new co-op? That you'll never be good at anything? Of making the wrong decision?

Now think about this. What are you feeding more? Do you keep thinking over and over about whatever it is that you fear, or do you focus on God's perfect love and the plan and purpose He has for your life? When you begin to understand that God's love for you is perfect, without flaw or blemish, it means you can trust Him. And if you can trust God, knowing He has a plan and purpose for your life, there is nothing you can't face.

So let love rule! Let God's love for you dominate your feelings, peer pressure, and fear.

IN YOUR OWN WORDS

1. What does love overcoming fear look like to you? What actions can you take to walk in love?

2. Write an acrostic poem using the word *love.* (An acrostic is a form of writing where each letter of a certain word begins a new word, creating an expression or name when read in sequence. For example, FEAR = False Evidence Appearing Real.)

SOMETHING TO THINK ABOUT

The LORD is my light and my salvation—
whom shall I fear?
The LORD is the stronghold of my life—
of whom shall I be afraid?

—Psalm 27:1, NIV

BUT I DON'T WANT TO!

KEY VERSE

This is my command—be strong and courageous! Do not be afraid or discouraged. For the LORD your God is with you wherever you go.

Joshua 1:9, NLT

The church I attended growing up was known for their theatrical productions of faith-based musicals. We're talking as big and wow as Broadway. Hundreds of people in the cast. A full orchestra. Live animals. Incredible sets and costumes. Thousands would attend and even more would tune in when it was broadcast on TV.

I loved watching those plays but I never wanted to be in them. I wasn't comfortable speaking in public. My parents took notice of this early on. And, much to my horror at first, they started signing me up for every activity in which I needed to stand in front of a crowd and talk, even sing. They made me pray out loud in front of others. They made me give presentations at science fairs. They made me try out for church plays. That was the worst. I remember one of my first auditions.

I was so nervous. I stood at the center of a huge platform. The judges sat in front of me, stone faced, waiting to see me perform. A spotlight beamed straight at me. It was so bright I could hardly see. And without even saying my name and my age, which I was supposed to do before my audition, I mumbled some poem my parents made me memorize. I don't know if the judges even understood a word I said. I'm pretty sure I kept my head down the entire time.

What came next was even worse. I had to sing. I don't know if you've ever heard me sing, but I'll say it's definitely not one of my gifts. I sang a few lines of some song, my voice cracking here and there, fumbling out of pitch. When I was done, I practically ran off the stage in embarrassment. (Side note: I ended up getting the part of Superman, which is ironic considering my scaredy-cat audition.)

Mom and Dad weren't being mean or setting me up to fail. They were helping me overcome my fears. When you are constantly challenged to go outside your comfort zone, eventually you become comfortable there. You learn to rely on God to help get you through. You grow as a person.

When I was thirteen, as part of a mission outreach, my youth group visited an arcade. About thirty young people from town packed the place, playing Skee-Ball, pinball, and air hockey. One of the leaders asked us kids, "Who wants to get up and preach?" No one said a word. I volunteered. I didn't necessarily want to or feel inspired, but no one stepped up. At the same time I said yes, my nerves broke out. *What if I forget what I'm supposed to say? What if my words come out wrong? What if no one listens? What if they laugh at me?*

When it was time to talk, even as fear weighed heavily on me, I spoke from the heart. I may not have come across as a great speaker, but I was sincere. And if I remember correctly, a handful of people accepted Jesus as their Lord and Savior.

One of the youth group leaders asked me to give a testimony of that experience later that night in front of hundreds of youth group kids. Again, I was nervous and unsure. I didn't want to do it. But I did. Later, I was asked to give the same testimony at church the following Sunday to a congregation of thousands. It made me feel uncomfortable, but I did it.

Funny, today I talk all the time at different events in front of small crowds and big ones. And while I still get nervous every now and then because I want to do well, I love sharing what God places on my heart.

If you're faced with a task or a project or even feel in your heart that God is asking you to do something that might make you feel uncomfortable, do it. Take a chance. Befriend that person. Volunteer for that club. Try out for that sport. Stand up for someone who is getting picked on. Give that presentation. Sing that song. Force yourself to do something hard. Remember, "God is with you wherever you go."

With Him, you can be strong. You can be courageous. And you can do the hard stuff.

IN YOUR OWN WORDS

Write about a time you did something outside of your comfort zone. How did it turn out?

SOMETHING TO THINK ABOUT

The comfort zone is one of the greatest enemies of human potential. When people get into a comfort zone, they strive to stay in that comfort zone. . . .

You need the courage to continually move yourself in the direction of your biggest goals and ambitions. You need to be willing to face discomfort in order for you to grow.

—**Brian Tracy, blog post**

YOUR CHOICES MATTER

KEY VERSE

Dear friends, God is good. So I beg you to offer your bodies to him as a living sacrifice, pure and pleasing. That's the most sensible way to serve God. Don't be like the people of this world, but let God change the way you think. Then you will know how to do everything that is good and pleasing to him.

Romans 12:1–2, CEV

Life is full of choices. We decide a countless number of things each day. Like what to wear, whom to hang out with, what to watch, what to listen to, what to eat. Some choices seem small, inconsequential. But they matter. Big ones and little ones. Making good choices, ones that honor Jesus and defy insecurities, fears, or pressures, always lead to the best life.

As we get older, it seems our choices become more difficult. For most little kids, life is pretty simple. *What toy should I play with after breakfast? Do I want apple or grape juice?* As we get older, decisions become more important. *Do I go to that concert? Should I study or text my friends instead? Should I tell that special someone at church I like him? Do I pursue my dream or forget about it because others might think it's dumb?* Some choices are harder than others and require us to press on in spite of fear or doubt.

I remember a time growing up when everyone in my family was away on a trip except for my mom, twelve-year-old Peter, and nine-year-old me. One morning as I walked past my sisters' bedroom, I noticed something moving at the foot of their beds. When I stepped into the room to get a closer look, my mouth dropped to the floor. The movement I saw came from a huge rattlesnake, thick as a baseball bat and longer than the length of the beds. It slithered on the rug, the rings on its tale vibrating in warning. In a split second, the venomous creature slid out of sight. I couldn't tell where it went. "Mooommm!" I yelled, bolting out of the room.

My mother called one of our baseball coaches who was also a police officer and lived a few miles away. "Help! There's a snake in Katie and Christy's room. My husband's away. Can you please come over and get rid of it?" she asked with desperation. There was a long pause on the other end. "Uh, I'd love to, Mrs. Tebow. I really would. Problem is, I'm deathly afraid of snakes. Could you call someone else?" Disappointed, Mom reached out to a neighbor next. Unfortunately, he wasn't home.

That first man made a choice. He chose fear over helping out a friend in need. And instead of choosing to step in and fix the problem, he chose to put it in the hands of nine- and twelve-year-old boys.

Out of options, Peter and I made the choice to be the men of the house. We chose to get the job done. Armed with a hatchet and a shovel, we noticed movement under the blanket on the bed. In one swift move, we threw the blanket off the bed. Sure enough, there the threatening rattlesnake lay, slowly slithering around, daring us to come closer. Peter used his ninja skills to hold the snake down, and I chopped its head off with the hatchet. My brother and I solved the rattlesnake situation. We were able to do what a grown man wasn't, simply because we decided to. And the three of us slept soundly that night.

While I doubt one of your life choices will involve snake removal, I am sure of this: you will face a huge number of choices as you move through your life. Like what to do when you get into a fight with a friend, what to say when someone makes you really, really mad, or how to act when faced with an obstacle that stands in your way.

So how do you make the right choice? Pray about it. Seek guidance in God's Word. Our key verse suggests we "let God change the way [we] think." Sometimes it's hard to make a good choice, even though we know it's right. That's when we need to lean on Jesus for the help that He has promised to give. Remember, the key to the best life is to honor Him. And when we do this, we are sure to live at our best.

IN YOUR OWN WORDS

Think of a specific instance when you had a significant decision to make. How old were you? What was the situation? What did you decide to do? Who/what helped you form your choice? How did it change your life for the better or create a challenge?

SOMETHING TO THINK ABOUT

Two roads diverged in a wood,
and I—I took the one less traveled by,
and that has made all the difference.

—Robert Frost, "The Road Not Taken"

IT'S NOT ALL ABOUT THE DON'TS

KEY VERSE

Jesus understands every weakness of ours, because he was tempted in every way that we are. But he did not sin!

Hebrews 4:15, CEV

Don't lie.
Don't cheat.
Don't steal.
Don't do drugs.
Don't be selfish.
Don't be mean.
Don't waste your money.
Don't waste your time.

Some young people look at the Bible as a long list of don'ts. All they've heard growing up is what not to do, because it's wrong and because the Bible says so. Being reminded of a mile-long list of noes can be overwhelming for anyone. Ever think something like *It's impossible not to do all these things! Why even bother?* Some folks get so frustrated they give up quickly and start doing those very don'ts. I know many people who have rebelled in their faith because of this.

Living our faith in this world of great temptation is not easy. But it's a lot harder to do if we're motivated by the fear of messing up or the guilt that comes when we do, or if we're feeling like we're being forced to follow a don't list.

Over the years, I've learned that it's more important to focus on the rewards of walking with Jesus. What does it mean to be free? What does it mean to be alive in Christ? Here are a few things to think about:

- Before Jesus came into your heart, you were spiritually dead. Today, you are alive (see Romans 6:11)!
- Jesus lives in you (see Galatians 2:20).
- You are a new creation (see 2 Corinthians 5:17, NIV).
- Your sins are forgiven (see Acts 10:43).
- God will never condemn you (see Romans 8:1).
- You are created to have a full life, one with purpose and meaning (see John 10:10; Ephesians 2:10).
- You can overcome any obstacle blocking your way, even temptation, through Christ (see Romans 8:37).

- Jesus died so you don't have to be trapped by sin again (see Romans 6:6–7). This is what it means to be alive with Christ. This is freedom at its best!

See, the main goal of the Christian life is not to avoid sin. The goal is to be like Jesus, to enjoy life with God, and to invite more people to experience that life.

I love what one of my pastors recently said: "God didn't save you to keep you in a holding pattern until heaven." So instead of focusing all your energy on not cussing, not telling a lie, not clicking on that website, not doing something inappropriate with someone else, not cheating on that test, or not being unkind to the new kid in town, tune in to this remarkable truth: you are saved through faith in Jesus to do good things, amazing things (refer back to week 4 for a refresher).

Look, sin is real. Temptation is out there. We all struggle with wanting to do something that may make us feel good in the moment but in the long run will not help us live at our best. Here's a news flash: you are going to make mistakes. And guess what? So am I.

And now for the great news! The Bible tells us that if we confess our sins, God is faithful and just to forgive us (see 1 John 1:9). And God doesn't only forgive; He transforms! This brings to light the true meaning of grace. And this is what should motivate us to say yes to walking in faith and striving to be like Jesus.

IN YOUR OWN WORDS

1. Make a list of ten things you can say no to. (And not just what you've been told to say no to but things you know wouldn't lead to your best life.)

2. Make a list of ten things you can say yes to instead.

SOMETHING TO THINK ABOUT

The temptations in your life are no different from what others experience. And God is faithful. He will not allow the temptation to be more than you can stand. When you are tempted, he will show you a way out so that you can endure.

—1 Corinthians 10:13, NLT

Week 17

TRUST IN GOD, NOT IN YOURSELF

KEY VERSE

Trust in the LORD with all your heart
and do not lean on your own understanding.
In all your ways acknowledge Him,
and He will make your paths straight.

Proverbs 3:5–6

I was the quarterback for the Denver Broncos. We were playing a team that was powerful, fast, strong. The morning of the game, I was spending quiet time with God. Reading the book of Proverbs, I settled on our key verse: "Trust in the LORD with all your heart and do not lean on your own understanding. In all your ways acknowledge Him, and He will make your paths straight."

I couldn't help but park there for a bit. *What does it mean to trust in God and not trust in myself?* The writer of this scripture reminds us not to lean on our own understanding. What is our own understanding? It's what in our human ability makes us feel confident. Or powerful. Or strong. It's whatever we can boast about in ourselves that makes us think we can tackle by ourselves any obstacle that comes our way. For me, this meant my drive to win, my competitiveness, my athletic ability. As I reread this verse a few times, I realized I couldn't put my trust in those things. I had to put my trust in God.

So throughout the game, under my breath, I repeated this verse. I wanted to be sure I understood that my confidence rested in God alone, not in my capability to perform or to win. I personalized this proverb to make it clear. As plays were run, passes were thrown, tackles were made, and touchdowns were scored, I said to myself, *Timmy, trust in the Lord with all your heart and do not lean on your athletic ability.* Saying this over and over brought peace. I could handle the outcome, whatever it was.

I have to admit, I was pretty disappointed when we lost the game. For a brief moment a part of me thought, *Oh man! I thought God was going to come through!* And in that brief moment, the peace that had swept over me during the game disappeared. So I forced myself to get my heart and my mind back into that place of trusting God. I reminded myself that even though His plan was different than what I wanted, He's "got this."

It's tempting to trust in things other than God. There are a lot of options out there for us to choose. Some trust in their good looks. Some trust in their knowledge or education. Some trust in their popularity. Some trust in their talent. Some trust in their ability to sweet-talk others. But trusting things or people, anything other than God, usually leads to disappointment.

Sometimes we are faced with situations that really hurt and shake us to our core, like a family crisis. Trusting God with all our hearts doesn't mean our prayers are always going to be answered exactly how we want. Or that He will come through for us in the way we want. Still, we are called to seek Him. We are called to trust Him. We are called to lean on Him—and Him alone.

So whatever happens, in good times and bad, know that His plans are always best. And even in hard times, God will show you the right path.

IN YOUR OWN WORDS

1. Name something within yourself or some person you know in whom you place great trust.

2. Has that trait or person ever let you down? How can you begin to trust God more?

SOMETHING TO THINK ABOUT

For as the heavens are higher than
the earth,
so are My ways higher than your ways
and My thoughts than your thoughts.

—Isaiah 55:9

DARE TO BE DIFFERENT

KEY VERSE

God created man in His own image, in the image of God He created him; male and female He created them.

Genesis 1:27

Robyn was born ten weeks early, weighing only two pounds, ten ounces. She was lighter than two iPads and could practically fit inside her parents' hands. She was diagnosed with cerebral palsy, a neurological disorder that makes it difficult and painful to move, and doctors warned her parents that she would always have trouble walking. When she was three years old, she started walking with the help of a walker and knee braces. It wasn't easy, but Robyn was tough and determined.

Because of her illness, Robyn had to have many surgeries and weekly physical therapy. She's always in a lot of pain. Though this had always been her normal and she never thought of herself as different, when she was in seventh grade, a classmate made fun of the way she walked. "For the first time, I realized that a walker wasn't normal," Robyn says. "And when I looked in the mirror, I didn't see a teenage girl; I saw what I was convinced everyone else saw: a disability."

When I met her, Robyn was going through a tough time. She told me that the past few months had been particularly overwhelming. She noticed people staring at her all the time. It was a reminder she wasn't normal. I was heartbroken that Robyn felt she wasn't special, that she didn't fit in. I tried my best to encourage her. "Robyn, normal is average. Being different is what makes you special and can give you the courage to treat others special," I said, as her eyes brimmed with tears. "God loves you, and you don't have to worry about anything else."

I saw Robyn a year later. Boy, what a difference a year can make! She told me, "I have come to realize that my differences don't make me strange; they make me beautiful. Today, instead of seeing my walker as a problem or a hindrance, I see it as a platform to influence lives; it's a way for me to inspire others."

Though Robyn still uses a walker and knee braces to get around, though people still stare at her, this young lady is not bothered by being different. Robyn appreciates *not* being just like everybody else.

The book of Genesis tells us that God created each of us in His image. You and I are created to be so much more than normal. Being normal is safe. And easy. It doesn't require much work or effort or change on our part. But it always leads to mediocrity. When you strive to be just like everyone else, you never have a chance to be special. When you start to embrace and even celebrate how different God made you, you can begin to do extraordinary things. You can begin to see yourself through His eyes. You can begin to live in the uniqueness with which you were created.

Following the crowd is not a winning approach to life. In the end it's a loser's game. So if you feel discouraged because you don't look like everyone else, you don't talk like everyone else, you don't go to the same school as everyone else, take heart. You were created by God to be different, to stand out from the crowd, to walk in the unique purpose and plan He has for your life.

IN YOUR OWN WORDS

1. Describe a time you felt insecure or "less than" because of something that made you different or made you stand out from those around you. How could you come to see that something as positive and unique?

2. Write a prayer to God thanking Him for making you special. In this prayer, list five things about yourself that you are grateful for.

SOMETHING TO THINK ABOUT

Don't strive to be like someone else. Be who God created you to be. Be you.

Part 3

Others Matter

When our identity is grounded in God, we live differently. Our priorities change. Our relationships reflect this truth—or at least they should. We aren't desperate for attention because God fulfills all our needs. Instead of using people to make us look good, we learn how to be faithful friends. We treat others with love, respect, and kindness. We watch what we say. We apologize when we make mistakes.

In fact, one of the biggest ways in which we can become more like Jesus is through relationships with others. The next nine lessons will help show you how.

Week 19

CREATED FOR RELATIONSHIP

KEY VERSE

A person standing alone can be attacked and defeated, but two can stand back-to-back and conquer. Three are even better, for a triple-braided cord is not easily broken.

Ecclesiastes 4:12, NLT

When I was playing football for the Denver Broncos, I was the talk of the town. I had some good friends. I lived in a beautiful home. Oh sure, the critics were out there. And they had a lot of negative things to say, but generally speaking, life was good. When I was traded to the New York Jets, life changed.

Outside of practices and games, for the most part I stayed home. A lot. My family and a few friends visited every now and then, but I still felt lonely at times. My coaches and others wanted me to lie low, keep away from media attention. But in trying to do this, many times I isolated myself from others. I wasn't involved in a church community. I didn't reach out to others. I'll admit it was a pretty dark time.

Here's what I learned during that lonely season: we need one another. God is a relational God. He made us to be in community. He made us to live in relationship with Him first and foremost, and then with others. This is what the church is supposed to be. It's not about four walls and a pretty building. It's about the body of believers we do life with. What does this mean? We need friends who are going to have our backs, who are going to support us and share the truth with us in love. We need friends who can carry us when we're weak. We need friends we can count on.

Our key verse is powerful: "A person standing alone can be attacked and defeated, but two can stand back-to-back and conquer. Three are even better, for a triple-braided cord is not easily broken." This is God's reminder that we are not meant to do life alone.

Choose friends who will encourage you to live out your God-given purpose, those who have your best interest at heart. Think about this: Do your friends lead you into or away from temptation? Do your friends stick up for you when others make fun of you? Do your friends encourage you when you feel sad, or do they stop calling because they don't want to be bothered?

I truly believe that God places people in our lives for a reason. Some of my friends have been in my life since middle school. And though our personalities may be different or we might not have everything in common, my friends are loyal and trustworthy. And they know how to make me laugh.

Friends can . . .

- encourage us
- motivate us
- inspire us
- celebrate with us
- listen to us
- make us laugh

The benefits of friendship are endless. And there are many different characteristics that make up a good friend. God knows exactly what kind of friends you need. If you're struggling to find some good friends, I encourage you to pray about it. He will put the right people in your life. Don't be surprised if it's someone you least expect. It could be the loudmouthed athlete or the quiet kid who would rather read than play sports.

God knows what He's doing. And He knows the right person or two who can help you live at your best.

IN YOUR OWN WORDS

1. Write about a friend who has helped you through a tough time. What did your friend do or say to make you a better person? What is something you admire about your friend, and why?

2. Write a tweet about the characteristics of a great friend. Just like on Twitter, use 140 characters or less.

SOMETHING TO THINK ABOUT

I would rather walk with a friend in the dark than walk alone in the light.

—Helen Keller, quoted in *Helen and Teacher*

Week 20

WHAT KIND OF FRIEND ARE YOU?

KEY VERSE A real friend sticks closer than a brother.

Proverbs 18:24, NLT

When I was fifteen, I went on my first mission trip to the Philippines. With Dad leading the charge, a group of us visited local hospitals, prisons, marketplaces, orphanages, and schools. We shared God's love with whomever we met. I'll never forget one remote village we visited on one of the country's thousands of islands.

As we walked through the village, hundreds of men, women, and children followed. They were curious about these Americans. With the help of some of the locals, we started gathering people together for a meeting at the high school. Everyone stopped what they were doing to come and listen to us talk. The place was packed. At least twelve hundred people showed up. I stood up and got ready to share a message about Jesus.

From the corner of my eye, I noticed three boys moving, slowly, from one side to the other, around the back edge of the crowd. They were far away, but as I began to talk to the crowd, I noticed they would take a few steps together, then stop and listen, and move a few feet more. It seemed they were being secretive, hoping no one would notice. Then, they cut behind a building and were gone.

I was blown away. It seemed everyone wanted to stay and listen to us talk. So why did these three boys leave? When the meeting ended, I set off to find these kids. As I turned the corner behind the school building, I noticed a bamboo hut. Then, a dark-haired head peered out of an opening. A boy walked out of the hut, smiling. *Yes!* He was one of the three.

I waved and said, "Hi there! I'm Timmy!" with a big smile on my face. He walked toward me and reached out his little hand. Wrapping his fingers around two of mine, he led me toward the bamboo hut where, I imagined, the other two boys were. As I crawled inside, one of the boys was lying down on a cot. The second sat beside him, stroking his arm. As I looked down at the boy on the cot, I noticed why he didn't get up.

His feet were on backwards.

My heart fell. As I fought back tears, we talked a bit before I asked, "I saw you guys while I was speaking. Why did you leave?"

Sherwin, the boy on the cot, answered, "Our school principal wanted to impress the Americans." He paused, looking down at his legs. As his eyes filled with sadness, he said, almost in a whisper, "And the principal said that I'm not very impressive."

My heart broke more. This boy should have been the first one seated in the first row. This boy should be loved, encouraged, lifted up—not dismissed or ignored like he wasn't good enough. In spending a few precious minutes with these three boys, I shared with them the love of Jesus. I told them that God had a special plan for them. I thanked the two boys for being awesome friends and told Sherwin that God created him perfect and that God thought he was very, very impressive. Finally, I was able to pray with these boys as they accepted Jesus into their hearts.

I learned so many things from that experience, but one that stuck out was how amazing these two friends were. These two boys stuck with Sherwin. They cared more about him than seeing these visiting Americans.

We need to be like them. We need to be a friend who is loyal, thoughtful, committed. We need to be there for our friends when they're sad, upset, discouraged. We need to stop thinking about ourselves and focus on how to be a good friend, the kind that sticks "closer than a brother."

IN YOUR OWN WORDS

1. Describe the character traits that make you a good friend. In what ways can you grow to be a better friend?

2. Write about a time you shared Jesus with a friend.

SOMETHING TO THINK ABOUT

A friend loves at all times.

—Proverbs 17:17

Week 21

AN ACT OF LOVE

KEY VERSE You shall love your neighbor as yourself.

Mark 12:31

Chris, the same kid I talked about in week 12, was short. Like, really short. Had been all his life. All of the kids in youth group that were his age and even younger towered over him like mountains. And many of them made fun of him for it.

"Hey, short stuff," they'd say while standing an inch or two away, looking down at him with sneers on their faces. Shrimp and Smurf were other names these bullies called him. Some even put their elbows on Chris and pretended he was an armrest. Oh, did I mention we're talking church kids? That's right. My friend was bullied by kids from Christian families. Kids who knew about Jesus. Kids who knew better.

My heart broke for Chris. I hated seeing him hurt. Whenever I would hear someone making fun of or playing a practical joke on him, I would rush to his defense. Whoever messed with Chris was going to have to deal with me.

As followers of Jesus, we are commanded to love our neighbors as ourselves. Matthew 7:12 says, "Treat people the same way you want them to treat you." If you wouldn't want to be bullied, don't bully someone else. If you wouldn't want to be made fun of, don't make fun of someone else. If you wouldn't want to be told you're ugly, bad, wear the wrong clothes, look weird, or talk funny, don't say those things to or about someone else.

And when everyone else is ridiculing someone or saying mean things about her behind her back, do the right thing. Stand up for that person. Love on that person. Defend that person. Show her the respect she deserves. Don't just do nothing.

Sometimes we think by not participating in bad behavior, we are doing the right thing. This is true in a sense, but Jesus doesn't call us to sit on the sidelines. He calls us to love others. And love takes action. Love doesn't do nothing. Love does something.

I like what Theodore Roosevelt, the twenty-sixth president of the United States, said: "Knowing what's right doesn't mean much unless you do what's right."

I made a lot of mistakes growing up. I had moments where I should have been more respectful to my parents. I had moments I should have shown more humility and less pride. I had moments I didn't tell the truth. But I have tried my best to stand up for the person I saw who was getting teased or pushed around.

I'll never forget the day our church youth group was preparing for a group photo. Chris looked upset. I had an idea. When it came time to gather together and squeeze into neat rows, I picked Chris up and held him while the camera flashed and clicked. My buddy looked just as tall as I did. And that day, he towered over all the other kids!

IN YOUR OWN WORDS

Have you ever been bullied? What do you wish someone would have done for you in that situation? How are you willing to do that on behalf of another person, to stand up for someone else?

SOMETHING TO THINK ABOUT

Each one of us has the ability to stand up for someone else. It's a way of life. Pay attention to opportunities where you can reach out to someone who is being shown hate.

TALK THE WALK

KEY VERSE

Don't use foul or abusive language. Let everything you say be good and helpful, so that your words will be an encouragement to those who hear them.

Ephesians 4:29, NLT

The conversations on the bus on the way back to church were loud and lively. My buddies from youth group and I powered on the volume as we bounced in our seats. One of the counselors on the trip had a knack for talking down to kids. He and I managed to get into a heated debate.

"Of course Michael Jordan is the best basketball player of all time," I started. I was confident in my opinion and had a ton of information to back it up.

He disagreed. He had strong opinions of his own.

Maybe because I didn't think this youth leader was the nicest guy to the young people he served, I wanted to put him in his place. I don't know. But I do know our conversation got ugly. I put him on blast. I got loud. *Real* loud. So loud, in fact, that all the talking on that bus just stopped. All eyes were focused on me.

"You have no idea what you're talking about," I said, my words burning with a lack of respect. I challenged his authority and his knowledge in front of seventy-some youth group kids. I didn't care that at one point he stopped talking. I just kept up my rant.

Though I believed I was right, I took my stance too far. By the time we got to church, the guy looked so embarrassed. Hurt even. And though my friends were high-fiving me in support, I felt terrible. *This is bad,* I thought. *I should not have been so disrespectful.* I was ashamed. I had let God down.

Every single person on this earth is worthy of being treated with dignity and respect. The Bible is full of commands to respect and submit to authority (see Romans 13), to honor others (see 1 Peter 2:17), to be humble and esteem others (see Philippians 2:3). That day, I didn't do any one of these things. I wish I could tell you today that I apologized to that counselor. I sure wish I had.

I'm a competitive person by nature. That's just how God wired me, which is a good thing. It's helped me face and overcome obstacles on and off the field. But there's a downside. Sometimes I want to win so badly, whether a game or an argument, that I end up unintentionally hurting someone else. I can't tell you how many times I've played the game Mafia with my siblings or a Madden video game with my friends, only to watch whoever I'm playing with stand up and walk out of the room because my competitive attitude got in the way of having a good time.

In the spirit of competition, I can talk smack, and take just as much, during a game or debate. And when it's over, I can walk away as if nothing ever happened. But not everyone can. I have to be mindful that what I say in the heat of the moment can hurt someone else.

I have to remind myself sometimes that winning isn't everything. That it's okay just to have fun. And that tearing someone down, even if I don't mean it, is never worth a win. As Christians, we need to be sure our words and the attitudes behind them are filled with grace, kindness, respect.

Now this doesn't mean we can never cut up with our friends; it just means we need to be aware that others matter more than being first, more than scoring a touchdown, more than hitting a home run, more than being the last player standing.

And more than having the last word.

IN YOUR OWN WORDS

Describe a time you got into an argument with someone. What did you decide to do? What good, if anything, came from it? What lesson did you learn in the process?

SOMETHING TO THINK ABOUT

Words—so innocent and powerless are they, as standing in a dictionary; how potent for good and evil they become to one who knows how to combine them!

—Nathaniel Hawthorne, quoted in *Nathaniel Hawthorne and His Wife: A Biography*

FIRE STARTER

KEY VERSE

Likewise, the tongue is a small part of the body, but it makes great boasts. Consider what a great forest is set on fire by a small spark. The tongue also is a fire, a world of evil among the parts of the body. It corrupts the whole body, sets the whole course of one's life on fire.

James 3:5–6, NIV

We lived on a farm, and that meant there was always a certain amount of excitement around the house. From hanging off of rafters in the barn or playing baseball with a basketball, we wound up with a lot of bumps, bruises, and even broken bones. The realities of farm life kept things interesting.

One time, as the weeds were growing haywire in the pasture, Dad decided to start a controlled burn to get rid of them. This is a normal and even a necessary occurrence on farms. Apparently *controlled* is in the eye of the fire starter, especially when you don't call the forestry department to forewarn them.

We knew something went wrong when Dad rushed into the house, frantic. "Help! I need everyone's help!" he yelled in a panic. Turns out, the pasture was on fire and moving fast toward the woods. If it got that far, it could spell disaster for us and for our neighbors. Mom and every one of my siblings ran out of the house carrying shovels and buckets of water. The fire hadn't yet reached the woods, but it had jumped into our neighbor's pasture. Staring at orange and red flames licking up toward the sky, we bolted into action, beating the edges of the fire with shovels while Dad tried to douse it with a gushing garden hose.

Through the grace of God and our efforts, the fire eventually died down. Though it had burned through the weeds in our neighbor's fields, his house was untouched by the flames.

Afterward, Dad took us all inside and used a teachable moment to have a brief Bible study on James 3. We huddled around the kitchen table, our drenched clothes stinking with the smell of smoke, our faces smudged with black. "Just like a small spark can cause a big fire," Dad said, "the smallest part of the body, the tongue, can cause great damage when we do not control it. A wrongly chosen word can hurt a reputation, alienate a friend, or break a heart."

Has anyone ever spread a rumor about you? Did you ever say something to a friend about someone else that wasn't true? Have you ever played the game Telephone in real life? You know, where a message is shared down a line of people and the final message is completely different from the original? This is gossip. And this is what happens when we don't tame our tongues.

Some people like to listen to rumors. Others like to spread them. We may do this because we like to be in the know or because saying something not nice about someone else makes us feel better. Whatever the case, if we're not careful, our tongue can ignite an uncontrolled fire that can harm someone else.

If you hear a rumor about someone else, stop it from going any further. Don't repeat it. You can also turn that conversation into something positive. Say something nice about that person. Show some grace. That's a sure way to honor God and fan the flames of love.

IN YOUR OWN WORDS

1. Think over conversations you've had with friends. Was there a time or two when you shared false or second-hand information? Describe the conversation. What should you have done instead?

2. Have you ever been the subject of gossip? Describe the circumstance and how it made you feel. How does this motivate you not to do the same thing to someone else?

SOMETHING TO THINK ABOUT

If someone is gossiping *to* you, the person will probably gossip *about* you.

LISTEN AND LEARN

KEY VERSE

A wise man will hear and increase in learning, and a man of understanding will acquire wise counsel.

Proverbs 1:5

Gosh! Coach is talking so much, I think. *Let's just get out there and start crushing already!* I'm pumped up and ready to hit the field. Our Pop Warner team is deep in the play-offs, a game or two away from hopefully clinching the national championship. It's half-time. We're in the lead. But I gotta admit, these guys are good. And they look like giants, though they're in the same age and weight class as we are. Hard to believe that when half of them have faint moustaches. Still, we are fighting hard.

"Keep your eyes open. Fight for every inch of that field," Coach yells at us players, as we huddle tight in the locker room. His eyes are on fire with passion. He's doing his best to make sure we understand how important it is to be on guard.

Halfway through his speech, I kinda check out. Half listening, I hear, as if miles away, Coach saying, "Hey, Timmy. Remember these guys are extremely fast. Don't get careless with the ball. Keep it high and tight." *Yeah, yeah, yeah. I've got it, Coach. I know what I'm doing. I'm going to win you the game.* But sometime during the fourth quarter, I get careless with the ball.

Coach calls a keeper, a play where instead of passing the ball to another teammate, I, as the quarterback, keep it and try to gain as many yards as I can. I take off down the field, legs burning with speed, feeling like I'm in the clear. I see the goal line. I'm almost there. I stiff-arm an opponent about to pounce on me, leaving him stunned on the turf. *A few more yards. Just a few more.* And then—*boom!* I'm tackled from the side. My body hits the ground hard with an echoing *thud.* The ball pops out of my hands. It rolls farther and farther away from me. I watch as if in slow motion as an opposing player scoops up the ball.

Game over. They win.

Read over our key verse: "A wise man will hear and increase in learning, and a man of understanding will acquire wise counsel." I didn't hear and increase in learning when I was huddled with my teammates in the locker room. I stopped listening to my coach. I thought I knew it all. I thought I got it. But really, I was a fool.

The book of Proverbs teaches a lot on wisdom, which is different than being smart or knowing a lot about different things. Charles

Spurgeon, a great preacher, once wrote, "Wisdom is, I suppose, the right use of knowledge. To know is not to be wise. . . . But to know how to use knowledge is to have wisdom."*

One of the most important ways to become wise is to listen. Admit you don't know everything. Seek to learn from your parents, your teachers, your coaches, your youth group leaders. Many times God will speak to us through the godly wisdom of others, those who know, love, and live for Him.

Being willing to listen doesn't mean you're dumb or weak. It means you are making the choice to grow stronger in wisdom. It means you are seeking to be more like Jesus, which is always the end goal.

* Charles Spurgeon, "The Fourfold Treasure" (sermon 991, Metropolitan Tabernacle, Newington, London, April 27, 1871), www.spurgeon.org/sermons/0991.php.

IN YOUR OWN WORDS

1. What's the difference between hearing someone and listening to the person?

2. What's the best advice you've ever received? Share the outcome if you followed that advice—or if you didn't follow it.

3. Is it sometimes hard for you to receive advice from others? Why do you think that is?

SOMETHING TO THINK ABOUT

Get all the advice and instruction
you can,
so you will be wise the rest of your life.

—Proverbs 19:20, NLT

SAYING "I'M SORRY" . . . AND MEANING IT

KEY VERSE

And "don't sin by letting anger control you." Don't let the sun go down while you are still angry.

Ephesians 4:26, quoting Psalm 4:4, NLT

I sit at the kitchen table. I want to be anywhere else but here. Mom points to a page in the open math book before us. It's filled with *x*'s and other variables and negative numbers and equations that just make my head spin. Mom is trying patiently to explain an algebra formula, but I'm miles away. I have no idea what I'm doing. Out of frustration and filled with pent-up energy from not getting these math problems, I start playing with my pen.

"Focus, Timmy," she says. "If the sum of two numbers is eighty-three and x is greater than . . ."

Her voice starts trailing off as I twirl the pen on the table. Faster. Faster. I'm totally engrossed in this spinning pen. It turns with remarkable force. And suddenly . . . *Bam!*

"Timmy!" Mom shrieks, as the spinning pen shoots off the table like a missile from a launch pad. Straight into the dead center of her eye.

I gasp with horror. Mom clutches her eye in obvious pain.

"It was an accident! It was an accident!" I say over and over. I hope I'm not going to get in too much trouble.

Mom is hurting. She runs off to the bathroom, clutching her eye.

When she comes back, I notice her wincing and blinking uncomfortably. My heart gets heavy. Before she has a chance to say anything to me, I break down. "I'm so sorry, Mom," I say, tears in my eyes. "I didn't mean to hurt you." Mom graciously forgives me.

You know what the problem was? I wasn't totally sorry. Instead of apologizing from the heart, I kept saying it was an accident. This way, I avoided responsibility. You know, the whole "It's not my fault" bit. But the fact was, it was my fault! I was responsible. And I owed her a heartfelt apology which I eventually gave.

The words *I'm sorry* can be the hardest to say, though. I think that's kind of ridiculous since we're imperfect people. I mean, we are going to mess up. We're going to make mistakes. We're going to hurt people, even unintentionally.

Ever borrow a sibling's jacket or video game without asking? Ever say in the heat of the moment something hurtful that you really didn't mean? Ever do something stupid, without thinking, that made someone else feel bad? My guess is that we've all said "I'm sorry" a bunch of times and that there are more to come.

If we mean it when we say "I'm sorry," do you know what that does for us? It keeps our hearts tender. Not weak, just open to God shaping us into the young men and women He has created us to be.

With five kids in my family, all of whom have bold and competitive personalities, we said "I'm sorry" and "I forgive you" a lot during our growing-up years. Our parents made it clear that we were never to go to bed angry, like our key verse suggests. They understood that not apologizing and not forgiving leads to a hardened heart.

Ever leave a dirty plate out after breakfast? What happens by dinnertime? The leftover breakfast on the plate is as hard as a rock. You have to scrub and scrub and scrub that grime off with a lot of muscle. If you had washed the plate right away, however, the remaining crumbs are much easier to wipe away.

When we know whose we are, we must let God mold our hearts. One way this happens is by being humble, being quick to apologize, and being sincere about it. When we are humble in our relationships, we show others we really care. That we love them. Not only do we grow as individuals when we do this, our relationships with others can grow as well.

IN YOUR OWN WORDS

Write a news article about the last time you had to apologize to a friend. Include what happened that merited the apology, who was involved in the situation, where the event took place, the conversation that took place, and the end result. Conclude the article with your opinion of whether or not you could have done something differently/better. Try to use descriptive words.

SOMETHING TO THINK ABOUT

Instead, be kind and merciful, and forgive others, just as God forgave you because of Christ.

—Ephesians 4:32, CEV

Week 26

FAMILY MATTERS

KEY VERSE

How good and pleasant it is
when God's people live together in unity!

Psalm 133:1, NIV

Your relationship with your family is important. It sets you up for how you will handle and relate to others in the future. In fact, it's the first place you learn about relationships. I don't know what your family looks like. Maybe you all live together. Maybe you don't. But I do know that your relationships with your parents and, if you have them, your siblings matter.

Having two older brothers and two older sisters was at times awesome and other times not so awesome. On one hand, it was neat because they knew everything about me. I looked up to them. I could ask them for advice. I could learn from them. We made memories together. We got into fights and we fought for one another.

On the other hand, it was also annoying having siblings who

knew everything about me. They knew how to press my buttons. They knew my struggles. They knew not just the good things I did but the bad things too. Like if I talked back to my parents or told a lie, even a "white" one. While I always strived to do the right things, I didn't get it right all the time. It was easy to play nice at church, but we all knew who we were at home and in the car on the way to church.

Having siblings can be a great thing. It can mean you have an ally, a friend to trust, someone who is there for you, someone who understands. But in order to have positive relationships with your family, you have to work at it. Maybe you're lucky and it comes naturally to you. Or maybe you fight at times with your siblings. Maybe you think they are annoying. Maybe they think you are. While teaching you a bunch of ways to grow in your family relationships would turn this lesson into an entire book, I want to encourage you to think about it.

If you're super close with your brothers or sisters, great! If you're not but want to be, spend more time with them. Do more than just deal with or put up with them because they're family. Get to know them. Hang out with them. Ask them questions. See what they're about. Do your part in making your family as close as it can be. I understand this is not always possible. All I'm asking is that you give it a try. It may not be easy, but it will be worth it.

On that note, how are things with your parents? I get that this is not the easiest relationship to navigate. No family is perfect. No child is perfect. No parent is perfect. The Bible tells us to honor our parents (see Exodus 20:12; Matthew 15:4). What does this mean? We show them respect. We understand, or at least try to, that the boundaries or rules they set in place really are for our own good (refer back to week 2).

You might get along great with your mom or dad. Or maybe you're constantly frustrated with them because they just don't get you. When we try to approach our relationships with our parents with a good attitude, our family bonds grow stronger. And we learn a few things. We learn how to deal with authority. This is important when we go to college or get jobs. This also can help us deal with people when we are in leadership positions of our own.

One more thing. For most of us, when it comes to family, we will be in one another's lives for many years. We might as well decide that we want to have great friendships with parents and siblings we will spend so much time with. It's an investment in relationships that will, God willing, pay off for a long time in great memories and shared experiences.

Make your family a priority. Strive to be united with your brother or sister. Support one another. Respect one another. Be there for one another. Besides your relationship with Jesus Christ, you should make taking care of your family one of your top priorities.

IN YOUR OWN WORDS

List each member of your family you live with. List three ways you can love and honor each one. Take action this week and do those things!

SOMETHING TO THINK ABOUT

You don't choose your family. They are God's gift to you, as you are to them.

—Desmond Tutu, quoted in *Releasing Family Blessings*

Week 27

IF JESUS WAS YOUR BEST FRIEND

KEY VERSE

Greater love has no one than this, that one lay down his life for his friends.

John 15:13

We started part 3 of this book by talking about how important it is to be a great friend and to surround yourself with great friends. Now I want to talk about the best friend of all time.

Do you have a best friend? I'm not talking about the ten different friends you consider a bestie depending on where you are. You know, like a church bestie, a neighbor bestie, a shopping bestie. I'm talking about a tried and true best friend.

What does it mean to have a best friend? You share with him. You open up to him. You spend time with him. You lean on him when you're hurting. A best friend is someone who will go through the highs and lows of life with you.

Now think about this. What would your life look like if Jesus was your best friend? Does that sound weird, or does it sound cool? One of my heroes in the Bible, a missionary named Paul who wrote most of the New Testament, gives a pretty good picture.

Before he became a Christian, Paul was part of an extremist religious group that hated, even persecuted, Christians. When he met Jesus, he became a missionary, spreading the Good News throughout Asia Minor and Europe. But Paul paid a price for his conversion. He was beaten. He was stoned. He was put in prison multiple times. Eventually, he was killed for his faith.

Paul was in prison when he wrote Philippians. One of my favorite Bible verses is in this book: "I can do all things through Him who strengthens me" (4:13). Many scholars believe this prison held the storage system for all of Rome's sewage. Think of it as a holding tank for a giant Porta-Potty that served thousands upon thousands of people. Disgusting and smelly to say the least. Well, there Paul was, in chains, in what some say was a cell flooded with human waste up to his hips. I don't know about you, but if I was Paul, I probably would have been pretty upset about it.

But Paul wasn't. He wasn't bitter. He wasn't angry. He didn't shake his fist at God. No, he wrote verses about being able to do all things through Christ. And he wrote about joy, telling others how important it was to rejoice (see Philippians 4:4). Was he nuts? Out of his mind? A fool? No. He had a relationship with Jesus Christ.

And he knew that since Jesus was his best friend, he could handle anything. He had a reason to rejoice. He had a reason to be confident. He had a reason to live.

It's easy to serve Jesus when life is going well or when we're worshiping with our friends in church on Sunday morning. But what about when life takes a tumble? What about Monday through Saturday? How strong is your commitment to Jesus then?

There have been times in my life when I've put Jesus on a shelf only to pick Him back up the next day or two. I regret those times. Jesus is more than a symbol on a necklace chain. He's more than a positive quote. He's more than words on a page in a book written thousands of years ago. He's real. He's alive. And He wants to be your best friend forever.

So why would you want Jesus as your best friend? Simple. Because He died for you. Because He loves you. Because He has an awesome plan for your life. Because He will never leave you. Because if a friend, a sibling, or a teammate walks away, Jesus will be right by your side.

So the question is, do you want Him as your best friend?

IN YOUR OWN WORDS

Let's say Jesus was coming over to your house tonight for some pizza. Just you and Him. What would you talk about? Write down your conversation.

SOMETHING TO THINK ABOUT

I no longer call you servants, because a servant does not know his master's business. Instead, I have called you friends, for everything that I learned from my Father I have made known to you.

—John 15:15, NIV

Part 4

Live Bigger

Who we are has to be bigger than what we do. Than what we look like. Than where we live. Than whom we know. Than how many followers we have on social media or how many Likes we get.

When we are rooted in whose we are, we realize we can live with purpose. And when we live with purpose, we can make a difference that leaves a lasting impact.

In these final nine lessons, I talk about what it means to live bigger. God wants to use you. But you need to accept the call. You need to say yes. Say yes to sharing the Good News of Jesus. Say yes to encouraging a friend. Say yes to using whatever talent God has blessed you with for His kingdom. It's amazing what can happen when you step out in faith and choose to live and make choices that have a lasting impact.

Week 28

NEVER TOO YOUNG TO THINK BIG

KEY VERSE

Don't let anyone think less of you because you are young. Be an example to all believers in what you say, in the way you live, in your love, your faith, and your purity.

1 Timothy 4:12, NLT

I may have had some successes on the field, but I want to live bigger than that. My life is more than sports. More than football. More than baseball. I want my life to speak louder than records, than what team I'm playing for, than praise from others. I want to live in a way that outlives me. I want my love for God and for others to take center stage.

Life is not just about having fun or getting good grades or making the varsity team, although there's nothing wrong with these things. But as Christians, God has called us to live bigger. He desires us to live in a way that makes a difference in the life of one person, or of many.

You may be thinking, *But, Timmy, I'm just a kid. What can I do?* Let me tell you something, friend. Through God, you can do a lot! The Bible even tells us not to let how young we are get in the way of being an example: "Don't let anyone think less of you because you are young. Be an example to all believers in what you say, in the way you live, in your love, your faith, and your purity."

The second part of this scripture is a clue to what it means to live bigger. It has to do with making the choice to live in a way that reflects Jesus in all we do. It has to do with doing the right thing. It has to do with making decisions that will honor God. It has to do with serving others. (Throughout the next eight weeks I'll share ways you can live bigger.)

Living bigger is not about being perfect. And we don't have to become a preacher or be a missionary in a country on the other side of the world. We need to let Jesus shine in what we say, how we live, what we do, how we love, and how we share our faith. Right where we are. And you're never too young to do this.

When I was ten years old, I led a little boy to the Lord. I'll never forget that moment. Even as a kid, it changed my life. I went with my youth group to a community outreach event in an inner city. Christy, one of my sisters, went with me. We noticed a boy all by himself.

"Go talk to him," Christy encouraged.

I was hesitant. "But I'm not sure what to say."

"Just be yourself," she replied. "And tell him how Jesus changed your life."

Even though I was somewhat nervous, I introduced myself to the boy. We took a seat on a bench outside of the recreation center and started talking. I was wearing a bracelet with multicolored beads. Every color represented one part in the path to salvation. I went through each bead with him and explained how much Jesus loves him and came to this earth to die for him so he could live forever with Jesus. We prayed together. And a few minutes later, that little boy accepted Jesus as his personal Savior. It was an incredible moment.

I didn't know all the theology around my faith. I didn't know all the Scriptures. And I didn't share my faith in the most eloquent way. But I did it. And a little boy came to know Jesus that day.

You may be young, but you can do amazing things! You may not have all the answers, but you can always point someone to the One who does.

One of the most important things is to remember that living bigger isn't just on us. It's on God too. Whatever we do in word or in deed, God is there beside us, helping us every step of the way. Remember when David chose to stand up and fight Goliath? Well, he wasn't able to do it in his own strength. He needed God to come through on his behalf. David had faith. David said yes. And God did the rest.

Are you willing to do bigger things in your life than just play video games or get the most people to follow you on social media? Are you willing to strive for more? Are you willing to get in the ring? Are you willing to fight for something or someone? Are you willing to invite a friend to church? Are you willing to pray for a stranger? Are you willing to do something that takes faith and courage?

I promise you this: if you are willing, God will always give you an opportunity. Question is, will you take it?

IN YOUR OWN WORDS

1. Think about the phrase *live bigger.* Write down six ways that can help to define what these words mean. If you're feeling creative, take one or two of these statements and make a poster or drawing out of it.

2. How do you feel about sharing your faith? Is it something you are comfortable doing, or do you find yourself feeling nervous or awkward? What are some things you can do to share Jesus in a bigger way?

SOMETHING TO THINK ABOUT

Someone is always looking up to you. And their life will be changed because of you. How will you choose to live?

Week 29

INVEST IN THE BEST

KEY VERSE

Do not store up for yourselves treasures on earth, where moth and rust destroy, and where thieves break in and steal. But store up for yourselves treasures in heaven, where neither moth nor rust destroys, and where thieves do not break in or steal.

Matthew 6:19–20

What are your priorities? Getting good grades? Hanging out with friends? Playing baseball?

What do you think about the most? The cute boy or girl in your co-op? How the season of your favorite TV show is going to end?

What do you think about when you envision the future? What college you'll attend? Whom you're going to marry? How much money you'll make?

While none of these things are necessarily wrong for you to

think about, I want to encourage you to also invest your thoughts in eternal things. Why? Because most of what we focus on in this life doesn't last. In fact, the Bible even tells us this in our key verse.

See, fashions fade. Opinions change. Friends come and go. Money too. What matters is living for Jesus. Loving God and loving others. Making a difference. These are heavenly treasures we need to start storing up.

In week 20, I talked about Sherwin, the amazing little boy I met on my first mission trip to the Philippines. On another trip when I preached to seven hundred students at a local high school, a minute after I started sharing the message of Jesus, it started to rain. I'm not talking a light drizzle. A torrential downpour started flooding the ground! The storm was so bad, the electricity went out. About a hundred students started walking out, but the rest stayed behind. Without a working microphone, I was grateful God gave me a loud voice. I began to preach using what Mom would call my outside voice. When I finished, five hundred high school students walked forward in the pouring rain to receive Jesus as their Savior!

After that life-changing experience, I knew I wanted to return to the Philippines. So when it came time to make my summer plans the following year, I had an idea. I told my parents that instead of going to football camp or playing summer basketball, I wanted to spend three weeks serving others in the Philippines.

Now, you need to know I didn't always give up certain activities for mission trips. But when I did, I gained so much more than what I imagined. Going to football camp wouldn't have necessarily been a waste of my time. Nor playing summer basketball. If I did those things, I would have continued to hone my athletic skills. And there's nothing wrong with getting better at the talents God gives us. Thing is, I preferred to invest that summer in something that had eternal significance. I knew I could make a difference in the lives of the young people in the Philippines. I knew God could somehow use my efforts, however big or small, to accomplish a greater good.

Sometimes we think we need to be in ministry to invest in things that last. But we can serve God anywhere! We can make a lasting impact on others in our neighborhood, at church, even at the local grocery store.

Think about this. What do you want to be known for? Do you want to be known for all the shows you watch on Netflix? For playing video games? For keeping up with the latest trends? For what a great singer, athlete, or musician you are? Or do you want to be known for making a difference in the kingdom of God?

Now think about how you spend your time. Think about where you invest your energy, your talents, your resources. How do these things fit in the big picture of eternity? Will they last? Are they important? Do they matter?

Living for Jesus means having a different perspective on how to live. When we do things that glorify God—whether serving others, taking time out of our day to pray for another, or doing something nice for someone else—it pleases God. And if it pleases Him, it matters.

IN YOUR OWN WORDS

Think about the word *eternity.* Write an acrostic poem about what it means to you.

SOMETHING TO THINK ABOUT

Only life lived for others is worth while.

—Albert Einstein

Week 30

SHOW LOVE, SHOW JESUS

KEY VERSE Three things will last forever—faith, hope, and love—and the greatest of these is love.

1 Corinthians 13:13, NLT

Remember Daddy's Dollars, which I wrote about in week 6? After a few years of doing my best to get the most dollars and earning money by doing things like helping my neighbor with his chicken farm, I had a lot of money saved by the time I was about ten. At least it was a lot for a kid.

I learned quickly from watching some of my siblings that I should save the cash, not spend it. I'd seen too often one of them rush out to buy a cool shirt or something and then have little to no money left over. I had also watched my dad work tirelessly to help the people he served in the Philippines. Before I visited that country on a mission trip when I was fifteen, Dad shared with me his journey in that part of the world through photos and videos. I learned early on what a lucky little boy I was. Unlike some of the children Dad and his team served, I always had something to eat. I had a roof over my head. I had shoes on my feet. I had a mom and a dad. It broke my heart to see children who didn't have some of these things.

When I was around ten years old, I determined to use the money I had saved for good. The Bible tells us that faith, hope, and love will last for all time, and that the greatest is love. Is there a better way to show Jesus to others than to give, serve, or help them? This is a form of love. And this is something that will have an eternal impact.

While I was boy, I dreamed of one day making a million dollars and giving it away. And I always gave my dad some of my money to take with him to the Philippines. I wanted to help kids who didn't have much. And Dad would always come back from his trips and tell me story after story about how even my chump change was enough to buy a little boy or girl my age a pair of flip-flops, or a bag of food for the family, or even a Bible.

We live in such a me-focused world. We take pictures of ourselves all the time. We tell the world on Facebook and Instagram what we're doing, what we like, where we're going. We want all eyes on us. But that's not what we're called to do as Christians. We're called to be others-minded. We're called to love others. We're called to serve others. We're called to be like Jesus to a world who doesn't know Him.

We don't have to do this just by giving money; we do this by focusing less on ourselves and more on others.

- If you see someone who is getting picked on, stand up for that person.
- If you know someone is having a bad day, ask if you can pray for her.
- Pick first the kid who always gets picked last.
- Step outside of your church clique and be kind to someone who doesn't fit in.
- Smile at the lady who serves you lunch.
- Ask your elderly neighbor if he needs help with his garden.

If you're still stuck when thinking about ways to love on others, pray about it. Ask God to show you opportunities. And then pay attention.

Saint Thérèse of Lisieux was a nineteenth-century Carmelite nun. She didn't believe the only way to show her love to God and others was to do grand or heroic things, but through small ways. She said, "The only way I can prove my love is by scattering flowers and these flowers are every little sacrifice, every glance and word, and the doing of the least actions for love." She referred to this principle as the "Little Way," showing kindness and love in every deed or word, however small. We can all do that!

Even though we've been talking in these chapters about living bigger, we can sometimes live bigger by going smaller, offering little acts of kindness, small gifts of thoughtfulness, a few moments of our time. In God's way of life, these little ways really add up!

IN YOUR OWN WORDS

1. Write about the last time you did something for someone else that illustrated your love for Jesus. What did you do? What was the end result?

2. List three little ways you can show love this week to someone besides your family and friends.

SOMETHING TO THINK ABOUT

Beloved, let us love one another, for love is from God; and everyone who loves is born of God and knows God.

—1 John 4:7

WHAT'VE YOU GOT?

KEY VERSE

As each one has received a special gift, employ it in serving one another as good stewards of the manifold grace of God.

1 Peter 4:10

Growing up, I was always amazed at how smart my big brother Pete was. He was particularly skilled at electronics and computers. He was like the Tebow help desk. Got a tech problem? Peter was the guy to help solve it. My brother was really good at taking apart remote-control cars and putting them back together too. I'd watch him stare at a table scattered with screws and coils and a hundred different tiny metal and plastic parts. Before I knew it, he'd transform that messy pile of pieces into a car again, this time tuned up to work even better and faster.

When he was only twelve, Peter built his own radio station. Yep, you read that right. No one listened to it, but it went eight miles in every direction.

I remember getting so frustrated at times because that stuff came so easy to him but not to me. *At all.* But I discovered a way to work through the frustration of not being as good as Peter or my other siblings, Robby, Christy, and Katie. When those times of frustration and feeling "less than" came blasting my way, I learned that I needed to be thankful for the gifts and talents God gave me, not compare myself with the cool abilities of my brothers and sisters.

I talk a lot about God having a purpose and a plan for you. But you might read these words and feel like you don't have much to offer. Well, you do.

You + Jesus Can = Miracles. It's the very best kind of math!

In John 6, we read about a crowd of over ten thousand people (the Bible tells us there were five thousand men, so including women and children would increase the number greatly) who had been following Jesus, listening to Him preach the Good News. As it was getting close to dinnertime, these people were getting hungry. Without any food to feed the crowd, the disciples who were with Jesus got discouraged. Then, a little boy piped up somewhere in the masses.

"Take what I have," he said. "It's not much, but I'll give it to you." He offered the disciples five loaves and two pieces of fish.

What did Jesus do? He started giving it out to the crowd. And you know what? Not only was the food in this boy's lunchbox enough to feed every single person that evening, there were plenty of leftovers too!

It wasn't just enough. It was more than enough.

When we give Jesus what we have, it's always more than enough, because He is more than enough. Never feel like you don't have anything to give. He's not asking for what you don't have. He's asking for everything you do have.

Don't compare yourself to someone else and say things like "Oh, I wish I could be like her. She sings so well." Or "Why couldn't I have been born with his talent? He's the fastest runner on the team." Or "If only I were as smart as she is."

Think about what you're good at. Think about the unique traits that are hardwired in you. Think about what you love to do. Maybe you can think of cool ways to solve problems. Maybe you're a natural-born leader. You may have a unique way of relating to people. Maybe you're super compassionate, encouraging, or friendly. Maybe you're artistic or skilled at building things.

Instead of wanting to be like someone else, make the most of your talents. The Bible teaches us that "as each one has received a special gift, employ it in serving one another as good stewards of the manifold grace of God."

You can learn to live bigger by using what God has given you for His kingdom. Don't waste your gifts, talents, and abilities. Whether it's singing, speaking, serving, or working with numbers, use it to make an impact on this world. Because that's what God has called you to do.

I promise you this: God will use your giftings and abilities in His way and for His plan. It might be to impact one person or a million people. Rather than focus on trying to figure out or influence how He will make it happen, focus on Him.

IN YOUR OWN WORDS

Take another look at the story of Jesus feeding that huge crowd in John 6. Now put yourself in that little boy's shoes. Rewrite the story from your new perspective. If you were smack in the middle of thousands of hungry people, what would you have done? Would you think you had something to offer? How would the disciples and Jesus have responded?

SOMETHING TO THINK ABOUT

Talent is like electricity. We don't understand electricity. We use it.

—Maya Angelou, *Maya Angelou's "I Know Why the Caged Bird Sings"*

STAND UP FOR WHAT MATTERS

KEY VERSE Fight the good fight of faith.

1 Timothy 6:12

Most people know Eric Liddell as the inspiration from the epic and award-winning movie *Chariots of Fire.* Faith was a big deal to Eric, a son of missionary parents. The "Flying Scotsman" was also a great athlete. He played rugby and ran track at Edinburgh University. He soon became a star in both sports as a student-athlete, but he never let his successes go to his head. His faith came first and foremost.

Eric gave up rugby to focus on training for the 1924 Olympics in Paris. Several months before the games began, Eric discovered his top four races had heats on Sunday. He immediately made the decision not to run on that day, because he believed in keeping Sundays for Sabbath rest. He got a ton of flak for that decision. The newspapers wrote unkind things about him. Some even called him a traitor.

A few days after that Sunday, Eric ran in the two-hundred-meter race and won a bronze medal. Eric also competed in the four-hundred-meter race. He won a gold medal with a world-record time of 47.6 seconds. He was the first Scotsman to ever win an Olympic gold medal. Eric gave credit for his win to God.

This young man was more than an Olympic gold-medal athlete. A few years later, he moved to China as a missionary teacher. When the Japanese invaded the North China mainland and war broke out, Eric was arrested and captured as a prisoner.

Before his death at the age of forty-three, Eric took a stand for those around him by showing them the love of Jesus. He helped improve the morale of his fellow prisoners. He organized athletic games. He taught science to children. He helped those who were sick. He was known for being joyful, loving, and compassionate.

Eric fought the good fight of faith. He ran a good race and finished strong. His faith in Jesus Christ was always his first priority.*

I'm a big believer in the statement "If you don't stand for something, you'll fall for anything." What does it mean to take a stand? It's pretty simple. It's standing up for something or someone you believe in. Every single one of us has the power to do that.

Standing up is a way of life. Find a need and fill it. Love on people. Be generous with your time. Be a faithful friend. Be kind to strangers. Let the light of Jesus shine through you in what you say

* See www.ericliddell.org/ericliddell/biography and www.christianity.com/church/church-history/church-history-for-kids/eric-liddell-greater-than-gold-11634861.html.

and how you act. This is what it means, as our key verse encourages, to "fight the good fight of faith."

The stand you take may not be the biggest deal to the entire world, but it can be a big deal for one person. For instance, you don't have to feed all of Africa, but feeding one person can have more of an impact than you may realize. So can taking a stand for someone who is getting bullied.

I've taken a stand for many things, even a knee now and then. If you're not sure what to take a stand for, think about this: Do you know someone who is hurting? Is there a problem in your sphere of influence that you can fix? Is there a wrong you can make right?

Again, find a need and fill it. Do what's right. Stay true to your faith. Stand up for what you believe in. Ask God to put something or someone on your heart. Do something different. This is what it means to take a stand.

Taking a stand doesn't always require a ton of work, a huge effort, or a perfect strategy. You don't have to start a foundation or end world hunger. And it doesn't need to be this powerful moment where everyone in the room or in the world is watching. It only requires willingness.

IN YOUR OWN WORDS

Write a story about someone who took a stand for something or someone else. What happened?

SOMETHING TO THINK ABOUT

If you don't stand for something, you'll fall for anything.

—Original Source Unknown

DON'T GIVE UP

KEY VERSE Let us not lose heart in doing good, for in due time we will reap if we do not grow weary.

Galatians 6:9

Living bigger is not always easy. Whether you share the message of God's hope and love with someone, serve others who are less fortunate, donate your allowance for a good cause, or stand up for someone who is being mistreated, obstacles will come. Someone might make fun of you or dismiss your effort. Others might tell you to give up. You might feel like quitting. You might even feel you won't make much of a difference.

Have courage and keep trying. God can do amazing things. He may even inspire great change when you keep saying yes to the right things.

I think about black athletes, heroes who paved the way in sports.

There was once a time when black people were not allowed to play on the same fields as white people. Crazy, right? Before the 1936 Olympics, black Americans could not even try out for the games. But in that year, for the first time ever, eighteen young Black men and women, including Jesse Owens, were finally allowed to participate. These athletes stood tall and proud in the storm of racial discrimination to fight for what they believed in: equality. And they pioneered the start of the changing face of professional sports.

I think of Joseph Louis Barrow, later known as Joe Louis. This Alabama farm boy grew up to become boxing's heavyweight champion of the world in 1937. He kept that title for eleven years and eight months. Louis became a hero at a time when racial discrimination was more than just part of societal fabric; it was also the law.

I think of Jackie Robinson, the grandson of a slave. When Jackie integrated Major League Baseball on April 15, 1947, some hailed the event as the most monumental civil rights success since the Civil War. In *I Never Had It Made,* he wrote about his experience: "I remember standing alone at first base—the only black man on the field. I had to fight hard against loneliness, abuse, and the knowledge that any mistake I made would be magnified because I was the only black man out there."

Despite taking abuse and constant verbal attacks, despite being the butt of jokes and getting called terrible names, these individuals and other men and women after them never gave up. They remained steadfast in tough times. And they made it possible for amazing athletes like Althea Gibson, Muhammad Ali, Michael Jordan, Jackie

Joyner-Kersee, the Williams sisters, and many others to pursue their dreams.

Our key verse reminds us to never give up. Eventually, we will reap a reward. I don't know what the reward will be for you, but one thing I do know is that God has a plan and a purpose for your life. And if you're willing, He will use whatever platform He gives you to make it happen.

You might think of a platform as the place on which a musician performs or a pastor teaches. I like to think of a platform as a space in your life where you have influence over others, whether one person or many people. A platform can be your family, your circle of friends, your neighborhood. Your platform may not be playing sports or performing on a grand stage, but your purpose will always be to love God and to love others.

One more thing, please understand that doing the right thing is not a get-rich/popular/famous-quick scheme. But God will be proud of you. And in one way or another, He will honor you.

So open your eyes to opportunities to do something kind or nice for someone else. Give someone a hug. Send a text with an inspiring quote. Mail someone a heartfelt card. Tell someone how much you appreciate him or her. Donate some nice clothes. Make someone a sandwich. Lift someone's spirits with a kind word. Organize a Bible study. Use your talents for kingdom purposes.

And never, ever give up doing the right thing! You never know what will happen. The impact you make on one person just might change the course of tomorrow.

IN YOUR OWN WORDS

Think about someone you admire who didn't give up on his or her journey (for example, a grandparent who kept the faith even while struggling with a loss). Interview the person. Find out how he or she was able to persevere and the lessons learned during that time.

SOMETHING TO THINK ABOUT

When you get in a tight place and everything goes against you, till it seems as though you could not hold on a minute longer, never give up then, for that is just the place and time that the tide will turn.

—Harriet Beecher Stowe

Week 34

SAY YES

KEY VERSE

And without faith it is impossible to please Him, for he who comes to God must believe that He is and that He is a rewarder of those who seek Him.

Hebrews 11:6

When I was in the sixth grade, one of my goals was to bench press 315 pounds as a freshman in high school. I had heard of a senior at the local high school who had done this when he was a freshman. If he did it, why couldn't I? Some people thought I was nuts, but I liked setting goals that seemed impossible. It gave me something to strive for. I lifted regularly and worked hard to achieve this goal. And when I became a freshman, I did it. I bench-pressed 315 pounds.

On May 6, 1954, a twenty-five-year-old medical student named Roger Bannister became the first person in the world to run a mile in under four minutes, in 3:59.4 to be exact. No one had done this before. Some doctors and scientists even thought it was physically impossible for the human body to run that fast. It's funny: two months later, John Landy from Australia ran a mile in under four minutes. Since then, hundreds of athletes have achieved this feat. The record has been broken eighteen times since the first person believed he could do it.

Was Roger Bannister the fastest person in the world at the time? Is this why he was the first to run a mile in under four minutes? I don't think so. There may have been others who were physically capable of doing this, but he was the first to believe he could actually do it. Bannister set the standard and others followed. He believed it could be done and others started to believe it as well. (The men's world record as of this writing is 3:43.13.)

Do you believe God created you for a purpose? Do you believe God has a plan for your life? Do you believe God has called you to live bigger? To make a difference in this world? I want to encourage you to break your own "four-minute mile." Think about the dreams and goals that are in your heart. If you can't think of any, pray for God to put some there. Ask Him to help you see and think bigger. Maybe your dream is to share the message of Jesus with your entire neighborhood. Maybe your dream is to help feed homeless people in a nearby city. Maybe your dream is to write an inspiring book. Go for it. Give it a shot. Just say yes!

Think about Moses. God called him to lead the people of Israel into the Promised Land. But Moses did not accept the call immediately. He had a list of excuses why he wasn't the man for the job. Finally, even though he believed he was underqualified, Moses said yes. And through him, God did amazing things.

Remember David? This young man stepped up to kill a giant. He believed God could use him to defeat an enemy. You know how that story ended.

How about Gideon? God called this guy, who happened to be from one of the weakest and smallest tribes in Israel, to lead the nation into battle with the Midianites. The enemy army had about 135,000 soldiers. God told Gideon to fight using only three hundred men. Talk about being outnumbered! Even though Gideon was scared, he believed God would come through. And guess what? God defeated Israel's enemy using Gideon and a small-in-number army of only three hundred soldiers (see Judges 6–7).

These Bible stories are not fables. They are real. They actually happened. They are examples to us that when we believe, God can do amazing things. Did you know that God is pleased when we have faith? This is what the Bible tells us in our key verse. When we believe and depend on Him through faith, He is delighted!

So put five stones in your pocket.

Start setting goals.

Pray for opportunities.

Strive for more.

Raise your hand.

Say yes.

IN YOUR OWN WORDS

1. Make a list of three things that the world has said are impossible. For example, for centuries, people did not think that it was possible for humans to fly. The Wright brothers, through their invention of the airplane, proved many wrong. Next to those three things, list the ways in which God made the impossible possible (either by working through human beings or by miracles).

2. What in your own life do you believe is possible with God?

SOMETHING TO THINK ABOUT

Now may the God of hope fill you with all joy and peace in believing, so that you will abound in hope by the power of the Holy Spirit.

—Romans 15:13

Week 35

KEEP YOUR EYE ON THE PRIZE

KEY VERSE I press on toward the goal to win the prize for which God has called me heavenward in Christ Jesus.

Philippians 3:14, NIV

As I was growing up, each year my parents would ask my siblings and me to write down our goals. Mine were pretty much always the same (in no particular order): become a baseball player, become a football player, become a Navy SEAL, be a better brother. Most of them had something to do with sports. After I wrote them down, I would sit down with my parents and review them. Goals look great on paper but they don't matter if they just stay there. So Mom and Dad would help me figure out how to attack these goals. Together, we would figure out the specific steps that I would need to take and in what order to accomplish what I said I wanted to achieve.

Now, I didn't always accomplish everything I wanted. But I always noticed some growth. Working out regularly, for example, would help me get stronger, faster, better. It wasn't always easy. There were days I didn't want to do it. I might have been tired. Maybe I didn't feel good. But I forced myself. How? I kept my eye on the prize, whether that meant one day playing in the NFL or playing Major League Baseball.

Funny, a week before working on this lesson, I happened to be working out at a local gym. One of the instructors couldn't believe how I've disciplined my nutrition habits over the years. I don't drink soda. I don't consume sugar. I'm pretty strict with my diet.

"How can you say no to sweets?" he asked.

I explained it had to do with the source of my motivation. As an athlete, I have to fuel my body efficiently. I have to train. I have to work hard. I have to eat the right foods. I have to put into my body what will make it strong, lean, and fast. My motivation is being an excellent athlete. And as I work hard to make that happen, I have to keep my eye on that prize.

Look, it's not always easy to say no to sweets. But when I think about how saying yes to fresh veggies or lean protein helps my body operate at its best, it makes it a lot easier.

The prize of the faith life isn't just to get to heaven, although that's obviously a part of it. It's also to become more and more like Jesus. It's to have Him transform us day by day into the people He has created us to become. It's to share the Good News with people who don't know Jesus. It's to make a difference for Him. We can do this by growing in our faith, by being challenged in life, and by continuing to press on.

Think about whether you want to wake up a year or two from now being the same person you are today. Chances are, there are some things you could stand to change. We all can. Including me!

When I was younger, I was arrogant. I had to work on this over the years. And even though I've grown a lot in the humility department, it's still something I need to work on every day. I'm also a perfectionist. I'm always working hard to improve, to be the best. This is not necessarily a bad thing, but it can keep me from being grateful in the moment. I have to work on finding a balance between trying to be the best at whatever it is I'm doing and being thankful in the moment for what I have.

I find that whenever I'm reminded of my identity, whenever I remember whose I am, I am more motivated to change. Because I don't want to stay the same. I want to be like Jesus. I want my life to matter. I want my love for God and for others to show in what I do and what I say.

We're never going to be perfect in this life. But we can stretch and we can change. If you want to live bigger, you need to grow. No matter how many times you get knocked down or mess up, you need to hold on to God's promises. You need to believe that He has a better plan. You need to cling to His truth. And day by day, moment by moment, you will become more and more like Jesus.

IN YOUR OWN WORDS

Write down four areas in which you want to grow, like learning more about American history, studying a second language, or getting physically stronger. Now, for each of these areas, list the very first step you need to take to begin that growth. Create a plan for taking these first steps, and ask your parents to help you develop the next step, and the next, and the next, that will help you reach your goals.

SOMETHING TO THINK ABOUT

So all of us who have had that veil removed can see and reflect the glory of the Lord. And the Lord—who is the Spirit—makes us more and more like him as we are changed into his glorious image.

—2 Corinthians 3:18, NLT

Week 36

REMEMBER WHOSE YOU ARE

KEY VERSE Well done, my good and faithful servant.

Matthew 25:23, NLT

Not long ago, I was thinking about my goals and what I want to accomplish. I do this often. It helps remind me of what's important and determines how and where I spend my time. With a marker in hand, I stood in front of a giant whiteboard. I started jotting down ideas. *Write another book. Take a mission trip to the Philippines.* I noticed a recurring theme. That day I realized that my number one goal in life is to show Jesus through the way I live and the way I love. This doesn't mean I always do it right. This doesn't mean I always do it the best way. But all in all, it's something I strive for.

When we think about living bigger, it comes down to letting Jesus shine through us in what we say, how we act, how we lead, how we serve, how we interact with others, where we invest our time, what we do with our talents.

This is why faith matters. This is why it's important to nourish your relationship with Jesus. This is why it's important for you to pray regularly, to seek God's voice, to read His Word. Do you know why I start each lesson with a scripture? Because these words reflect the heart of your heavenly Father. This is what He says about you. You need to hide these words in your heart.

Don't just go through the motions of going to church or reading through a daily devotional with your family at the breakfast table. Dig into God. Press into Him. Soak in what He says. This will prepare you for the future. This is what is going to help you tackle obstacles that come your way. This is what is going to change your life. This is what is going to inspire and guide you to live bigger.

At the end of my life, it doesn't matter how much praise or how many pats on the back I've received from others. What I really want to hear is my heavenly Father tell me, "I'm proud of you, son" (my translation of our key verse).

While it makes you feel good to please people, it makes you feel fulfilled to please God.

God loves you. He has a plan and a purpose for your life. I challenge you to rise up and find the courage to be a little different, to do *something,* to open your eyes to ways you can honor God by serving and loving others. When you see people who need love, love them. When you see people who need prayer, pray for them. Be willing to do something. And know that God is with you. He's going to fight for you. He's going to show up for you. And He is never, ever going to leave you (see Hebrews 13:5).

Don't let life get in the way of choosing to live bigger. There is always something to do.

- Pay attention.
- Look around.
- Listen.
- God is speaking.

IN YOUR OWN WORDS

Reflect on what your life means, what it's about, what it stands for. Now write down the legacy you want to leave. What do you want to accomplish? What do you want others to say about you? What do you want to be remembered for?

SOMETHING TO THINK ABOUT

I believe the greatest legacy we can leave is a life lived for Jesus.

About the Author

Tim Tebow is a two-time national champion, first-round NFL draft pick, and Heisman trophy winner. After playing in the NFL for the Denver Broncos and the New York Jets, Tebow joined the SEC Network. In addition to his role on *SEC Nation,* the network's traveling road show, Tebow also contributes to a variety of other ESPN platforms. In 2016, he signed a professional baseball contract with the New York Mets. Through everything, Tim's true passion remains the work of the Tim Tebow Foundation, which he began in 2010. The foundation's mission is to bring Faith, Hope, and Love to those needing a brighter day in their darkest hour of need. The foundation is fulfilling that mission every day by serving thousands of deserving children around the world.

TIM TEBOW FOUNDATION™

To continue to fight for those who can't fight for themselves, a portion of proceeds from each book sold will be donated to the **Tim Tebow Foundation** to help further their mission of:

Bringing Faith, Hope and Love to those needing a brighter day in their darkest hour of need.

The foundation is currently fulfilling this mission every day by...

- Providing life-changing surgeries through the **Tebow CURE Hospital** to children of the Philippines who could not otherwise afford care.
- Creating a worldwide movement through **Night to Shine**, an unforgettable prom experience, centered on God's love, for people with special needs.
- Building **Timmy's Playrooms** in children's hospitals around the world.
- Fulfilling the dreams of children with life-threatening illnesses through the **W15H** program.
- Encouraging volunteer service to others through **Team Tebow** and **Team Tebow Kids**.
- Supporting housing, meals, medical treatment and education for orphans around the world though our **Orphan Care** program.
- Providing **Adoption Aid** financial assistance to families who are making the courageous choice to adopt a child with special needs internationally.

...simply put, Serving Children and Sharing God's Love!

To learn more about these initiatives and the continued growth of the foundation's outreach ministries, visit **www.timtebowfoundation.org.**